C. PETER WAGNER

STRATEGIES

FOR

CHURCH GROWTH

FOREWORD BY RALPH D. WINTER

C. PETER WAGNER
STRATEGIES
FOR
CHURCH GROWTH

*Tools for Effective Mission
and Evangelism*

GL
Regal Books

A Division of GL Publications
Ventura, California, U.S.A.

Published by Regal Books
A Division of GL Publications
Ventura, California 93006
Printed in U.S.A.

Library of Congress Cataloging in Publication Data

Wagner, C. Peter.
   Strategies for church growth.

   Includes bibliographies and index.
   1. Church growth. 2. Evangelistic work. 3. Missions—Theory. I. Title.
BV652.2.W34   1987   266   87-4458
ISBN 0-8307-1170-8

3 4 5 6 7 8 9 10 / 91 90 89 88

Rights for publishing this book in other languages are contracted by Gospel Literature International (GLINT) foundation. GLINT also provides technical help for the adaptation, translation, and publishing of Bible study resources and books in scores of languages worldwide. For further information, contact GLINT, Post Office Box 488, Rosemead, California, 91770, U.S.A., or the publisher.

Other Books in Print by C. Peter Wagner

Church Growth and the Whole Gospel (San Francisco: Harper & Row, Publishers, Inc., 1981).

Church Growth: State of the Art (Wheaton: Tyndale House Publishers, 1986).

Leading Your Church to Growth (Ventura: Regal Books, 1984).

On the Crest of the Wave: Becoming a World Christian (Ventura: Regal Books, 1983).

Spiritual Power and Church Growth (Altamonte Springs, FL: Creation House, 1986).

The Church Growth Survey Handbook, co-authored with Bob Waymire (Milpitas, CA: Overseas Crusades, 1980).

Your Church Can Be Healthy (Nashville: Abingdon Press, 1979).

Your Church Can Grow (Ventura: Regal Books, 1984).

Your Spiritual Gifts Can Help Your Church Grow (Ventura: Regal Books, 1979).

To

JOHN AND CAROL WIMBER

They have demonstrated how it can be done

Contents

9
How to Target Your Outreach

The Challenge of the World
The Challenge of the United States
Targeting Unreached Peoples
Research on the World's Peoples
The Cholanaikkans of India
Stimulating People Movements
Power Evangelism
Targeting the Cities
Targeting Whole Nations

173

Appendix: *The Lausanne Covenant*
197

Index
211

Bibliography
214

Foreword

As I began reading this book I was struck again by how open, straightforward, how easily read is what Peter Wagner writes.

Here is one of the all-time best teachers at work, and his book takes you right into the classroom. What you have in your hands is clearly the best, most balanced, most readable book on the crucial subject of world evangelization.

You know that he is not speaking out of thin air. You know that is not the first time he has dealt with all of these subjects. You know he is not hiding the viewpoints of others. Indeed you are impressed by how sensitive he is to the existence of other people with different opinions. He quite openhandedly takes up their points of view without any attempt to slight or blunt their arguments.

I have asked myself, "How could a book be so exciting to read and yet be so jammed with practical methods (tools he calls them)?"

This book won't do away with all of Peter Wagner's previous books on missions and church growth. But more than any other, it will give you a succinct overview with many leads on where to go next. It is an outstanding and stimulating contribution. No one would have been better qualified to make it.

Ralph D. Winter
U.S. Center for World Mission
Pasadena, California

Introduction

Strategies for Church Growth brings together for the first time many principles of evangelism and missions which have proved, through recent research and experience, to be practically effective in implementing the Great Commission.

We live in a day of accelerated world outreach. Never before have we seen so many people, around the world, acknowledging Jesus as Saviour and Lord and becoming responsible members of Christian churches. Never before has the harvest been as ripe as it is today. Never, therefore, has there been a more urgent need for sound theory and practice as we move out to reach the lost in obedience to Christ's command.

I have been teaching church growth strategy for over a decade and a half to American pastors in Doctor of Ministry courses and to missionaries and international church leaders in mission courses. Many have requested that the content of this teaching be made available on a wider scale through the printed page. *Strategies for Church Growth* is an attempt to do that very thing.

This is the first book which brings together, in a concise form, the latest research of the Church Growth Movement, the Lausanne Committee for World Evangelization, the U.S. Center for World Mission and numerous other contributors to a veritable explosion of evangelistic technology.

The book begins by discussing the biblical rationale for planning evangelistic strategy and for aiming our efforts toward church growth. Then it answers the question: Why and how should we prioritize our efforts? The book deals realistically with the delicate relationship between evangelism and Christian social responsibility, following the lead of the Lausanne Covenant.

Why is it that frequently so few of those who make "decisions" as the result of an evangelistic effort actually end up as responsible church members? The book discusses this issue in detail, suggesting that key corrections are needed in both our traditional theories and practices. This, unquestionably, is one of the most valuable and practical parts of the book.

The dynamic potential of informed and intelligent goal setting receives a prominent place, as it well should. But, what should our goals focus on? Modern church growth strategy answers: "On the world's unreached peoples." The so-called "people approach to world evangelization" is highlighted in the final chapter. It, in my opinion, capsulizes the state of the art in thinking about and planning for fulfilling the Great Commission in our generation.

No task could be more crucial. How to approach and plan for the execution of the task is the question of the day. *Strategies for Church Growth* is one attempt to address this key issue in a biblically pragmatic way.

C. Peter Wagner
Fuller Seminary School of World Mission
Pasadena, California

1
Why Plan Strategy?

Is church growth theory incompatible with belief in the sovereignty of God? Does adherence to church growth principles leave out dependency upon the work of the Holy Spirit?

An experienced missionary to South America once wrote an article about several problems he had encountered on the field that he felt compromised his Reformed faith. And one of those problems was church growth.

"I saw a spirit of deadness come over a mission," he writes, "as Dr. Donald McGavran's 'church growth theory' was experimented with." The author, who chooses to remain anonymous, is offended because, he believes, church growth "applies sociology to the realm of church planting and endeavors to discover by means of statistics, graphs, charts, and even computers, where ripe fields are and, therefore, where mission personnel should be placed." He also chafes against "an unhealthy emphasis on goal setting."

And all this because underneath lies a theological concern. He says, "It leaves no room for the sovereignty of God and the spontaneity of the Spirit's work."[1]

How Does God Do It?

I agree with the writer's concern. If strategy planning quenches the Holy Spirit, I too want nothing of it. Nor would I recommend it at all, if I had any reservations about whether strategy planning can be pleasing to God. God's work, I believe, must be done in God's way. However, I do not see this matter as an either-or but as a both-and situation.

Amen

The Divine Aspect

God and His sovereignty are good starting points. God is King and we are citizens of His Kingdom. It is essential that we, as citizens and subjects, know who the King is, what His purposes are for the world in which we live and what our roles are in contributing toward these purposes.

God has many purposes in the world today. Chief among them is His desire that men and women, alienated from God by sin, have their fellowship with Him restored. God loves people so much and wants this to happen so much that He gave His only Son, Jesus, to redeem us (see John 3:16). Through Jesus' death on the cross and His resurrection, the way to God has been opened.

God is "not willing that any should perish but that all should come to repentance" (2 Pet. 3:9). Jesus came "to seek and to save that which was lost" (Luke 19:10). The Good Shepherd leaves the 99 sheep safely in the fold to find the one which has strayed (see Matt. 18:12). God clearly wants His lost sheep found and brought back into the fold.

The Human Aspect

God, we have affirmed, is sovereign. Not only does His sovereignty allow Him to decide how He wants lost men and women brought into His Kingdom, but since He is also omnipotent, He obviously has the power to do it any way He decides. If He wanted to, He could devise ways and means of bringing people to Himself completely bypassing any human instrumentality.

But for reasons no theologian completely understands, He has chosen to use human beings as intermediaries. We are told that faith comes by hearing and hearing by the Word of God. But "how shall they hear without a preacher?" (see Rom. 10:13-17).

The very last words that Jesus spoke while He was on earth were those of the Great Commission. He told His disciples that they were to be His witnesses in Jerusalem, Judea, Samaria and to the uttermost parts of the earth. And then when He had spoken those words He was taken up out of their sight (see Acts 1:8-9). This, it seems to me, was done to impress His disciples, both then and now, that spreading the gospel should have a high priority in our service to God.

The Ordained Procedure

The human and divine aspects of spreading the gospel come together very nicely in 1 Corinthians 3:6 where Paul says, "I planted, Apollos watered, but God gave the increase." Every farmer knows that God and God alone can make a cauliflower or an apricot or a carrot. All the technology in the world is not sufficient to set up a cauliflower factory. But, as a biblical theology of agronomy would inform us, God ordinarily sees fit to produce the fruit when some human plants and someone waters. It goes back to Adam's fall when God said, "Cursed is the ground for your sake; in toil you shall eat of it" (Gen. 3:17). God gives agricultural increase when human beings work hard enough to create the conditions for production. In some sense, mysterious as it might be, God has established a similar procedure for world evangelization.

This is not to bring glory to the individuals who create the conditions because they do so only as God's instruments for the task. Paul says, "So then neither he who plants is anything, nor he who waters, but God who gives the increase" (1 Cor. 3:7). So long as we acknowledge that no human being can regenerate another person, we will give the glory to God. Only God brings a person from darkness to light and from the power of Satan to God (see Acts 26:18), but He sends people like the Apostle Paul as His means of making it happen (see Acts 26:17).

_____ Qualifications for Serving God _____

If it is true that our sovereign God chooses human beings as His instruments of spreading His Kingdom on earth, which individuals will He select? Not everyone qualifies. As I see it, there are at least six qualifications if men or women are to be useful to God in evangelistic or missionary outreach:

1. *People who know God.* In order to share the good news of salvation, God's chosen servants must be saved. They must know what it is to be born again, for without the new birth no one can even see the Kingdom of God (see John 3:3). The message God's servants are to carry to a lost world is the message of reconciliation to God through Jesus Christ. Such a message carries no authority from those who themselves have not entered into the family of God and thereby are not committed to Jesus Christ.

2. *People filled with the Holy Spirit.* Jesus drew His disciples to Himself and ministered to them for three years. They knew Him well. Part of His instruction to them was the Great Commission (see Matt. 28:18-20), their marching orders to carry the gospel to the lost. But knowing Jesus and His will for world evangelization was not enough. Jesus told them that before they could move out and represent Him in the world at large they must "tarry in the city of Jerusalem until you are endued with power from on high" (Luke 24:49). They obeyed Him and the power came on the day of Pentecost, as we read in Acts 2.

Different traditions have developed different terminology to describe this experience. Some call it "the baptism in the Holy Spirit." Others call it "the Spirit's anointing." Still others use the term "empowering." I myself prefer to call it "the filling of the Holy Spirit."

Being filled with the Holy Spirit is a constantly renewable experience. Just because I was filled with the Spirit last year does not necessarily mean I am filled this year. Just because I was filled yesterday does not necessarily mean I am filled today. Maintaining the fullness of the Holy Spirit on a continuing basis is necessary if one is going to be a useful instrument for God's service.

3. *People of prayer.* Prayer is communion with God. Through prayer we are able to know the details of God's will. While the Bible informs us of God's general purposes and His requirements for the Christian life, none of our names is in the Bible. As we get in touch with God through prayer we discover the specific role each of us plays in the Kingdom.

Prayer develops intimacy with God, and it takes time. Many who set aside time and give priority to prayer find the voice of God speaks directly to them. While such direct contact with the Father must always be tested against the written Word of God and confirmed by other members of the Body of Christ, it helps us enormously in being the kind of servants God wishes us to be.

In recent years I have grown appreciative of the gift of intercession that God gives to certain Christians. Yes, every believer ought to be a person of such profound prayer. This is our role.

But over and above that, those with the gift of intercession pray longer, with greater intensity and with more visible answers than does the average spiritual Christian. Spiritual gifts are given for the benefit of the Body of Christ as a whole, and one of them, the gift of intercession, becomes an important dynamic in the ministry of the Body's members, whether that Body is an established church or a Christian fellowship group.

God has given me several persons with the gift of intercession in the adult Sunday School class I teach. The result is a notable change in the quality of my teaching ministry compared to a few years ago when I did not have such intercessors. As my own prayer life is rather mediocre, I attribute much of what power my ministry has to the prayers of others with the gift.

4. *People committed to the Body of Christ.* Throughout this book I will reiterate that the ideal Christian life is oriented around three priorities: (a) commitment to Christ, (b) commitment to the Body of Christ and (c) commitment to the work of Christ in the world. The first three items on this list of qualifications for serving God relate to priority (a). This item relates to priority (b).

I hold a high view of the Church. I believe the Church is different from other human institutions in that it is not just an organization. Rather, the Church is also an organism with Jesus Christ as the head and every member functioning with one or more spiritual gifts. Those who wish to serve God effectively in the extension of the Kingdom must be firmly rooted in a local church. Why? Because God accomplishes His purposes in the world, not through Lone Rangers, but through committed communities of His people.

YES!

The Body of Christ provides spiritual intimacy, a system of accountability and numerous spiritual gifts which complement each other just as do the members of our physical body. Although my nose and my kidneys are not directly attached, they are members of the same body and my nose could not do its thing if it weren't for the kidneys. We are told in Romans 12 that the human body is a model for understanding how the Body of Christ operates. [2]

5. *People obedient to the Lord.* One of the tests of true discipleship is obedience. "Now by this we know that we know Him, if we keep His commandments" (1 John 2:3). God's ideal is that we give our bodies to be "a living sacrifice" (Rom. 12:1). If we want Jesus to use us, we must take up our cross to follow Him (see Matt. 16:24). All this adds up to total commitment.

Obedience to all Jesus' commandments is required. But in this book, we are concentrating on commandments directly related to evangelism and missions. Chief among them is the Great Commission. I will go into detail on the correct understanding of the Great Commission later, but here I am stressing that a willingness to obey is prerequisite to being used as God's servant for the spread of the gospel.

6. *People who are energetic and creative.* If the above five qualifications are properly in place, the sky is the limit for the use of human energy and faculties. God delights to lead His people. Psalm 32:8 is a popular expression of this thought: "I will instruct you and teach you in the way you should go; I will guide you with My eye." Many have

learned this verse by memory and quote it frequently.

Few, however, go on to quote the next verse which explains how God wants to do it. "Do not be like the horse or like the mule, which have no understanding" (Ps. 32:9). God wants to lead us like humans, not like animals.

What is the difference? Basically, humans are made in the image of God (see Gen. 1:26) and animals are not. Humans have reason, animals do not. Part of God's leading, then, consists of His using our powers of reason to accomplish His will.

Human Responsibility!

Nothing is wrong with or inferior about the human mind. Jesus told us to love the Father with all our heart and soul and *mind* (see Matt. 22:37). At this point the divine purpose and the human initiative for world evangelization come together. Provided God's servants have the proper relationship with Him, we are free to plan strategy using the methods and technology that will best accomplish the work of God in the world. The Father is interested enough in what we are doing to intervene, redirect and correct as necessary.

Key pt.

Major Components of Strategy

Having laid some biblical and theological foundations for strategy planning, we need now to recognize this fact: Strategy planning is not something that is optional in human life and activity. It is not something that adults do and children do not. It is not a practice of unbelievers and out-of-bounds for Christians. It is not a technique of Americans and not of Nigerians or Pakistanis.

Strategy is not an option in life.

Granted, not everyone thinks of strategy planning as such or analyzes it as I am about to do here, but we all do it. You do too. Every time you take a trip, cook a meal, play a game, plant a crop or call on a friend, you plan a strategy to do it. You planned a strategy to acquire this book and to find time to read it—at least to this point. If you think about it for a moment, you will easily recall a number of strategies you developed earlier today to accomplish various purposes.

As you consider your pattern of planning strategies, and analyze it a bit, you will see that each time it happened there were four major components involved:

1. *A person or people*. All human endeavor begins with human beings. Individual strategy may begin with one person. Group strategy will begin with the collective consensus of several people. If we are dealing more specifically with Christian work we find that God does not reveal His will in a vacuum, but to the people He has chosen to serve Him.

2. *Motivation*. Something must motivate the person or persons to do something. There must be a reason to undertake a task. It can be a felt need. It can be a good idea. Many times for Christians the prompting of the Holy Spirit or a vision of a great undertaking for God is the reason. The motivation produces the objective.

3. *Setting the goal*. Once the person is motivated, the very next step is to set the goal. A *goal* is more specific ✗ than an *objective*. I realize that management experts have different opinions on the use of the terms "objective" and "goal." It is a matter of semantics, but in the church growth field, largely due to the influence of Edward Dayton of World Vision, we have elected to use "objective" for the general idea of the long-range purpose and "goal" for the more measurable task or tasks at hand. Goals also can be long range, in which case setting several intermediary short-range goals is often appropriate.

No strategy should be planned before the goal or goals ⫶ eg. B.S.'s. are set. Thinking through specific goals is an excellent discipline which allows a person's time and energy to be invested efficiently. More about that later; for now, recognize that goal-setting can be a threat because, as soon as you set a measurable goal, you run the risk of failure. Some individual's personal insecurities will not allow taking such a risk. Some cultures place a high value on saving face, thereby making goal-setting all the more risky. One of the most comfortable things in the world is to have no goals, for then there are no failures.

Equally comfortable is to undertake some activity and later to define your goals according to what you happen to be doing. It is like the marksman who shoots the gun at the wall then draws the bull's-eye around where the bullet happened to hit. Unfortunately this rather evasive technique is all too common in Christian work.

4. *The strategy.* Once the goal is set, the strategy itself can be determined. What, then, is strategy? *Strategy is the chosen means to accomplish a predetermined goal.* When seen in those simple terms, it becomes easy to understand why strategy planning is so much a part of daily life.

Some insist on differentiating between strategy and tactics. Such a distinction is common in military science. Strategy is the overall process, while tactics are the various activities which contribute to the strategy. I have nothing against separating the two terms if it is helpful to do so. For myself, I have not found it useful and, for that reason, I usually call the whole thing strategy. Overcomplicating the matter, I find, tends to block some people's understanding.

Choosing the Appropriate Strategy

Many choices have to be made in planning strategy. When

you have discovered an appropriate strategy for one situation you cannot assume it will always work in another situation, although some strategies can be transferred, if the goal and circumstances are nearly identical. For example, certain situations in a baseball game indicate that the best strategy is clearly for the batter to bunt, and almost invariably a bunt will be attempted. But change the circumstances slightly and the decision on whether to bunt becomes much more difficult. Likewise, some evangelistic methods may work very well in a given situation, but they may be next to useless when circumstances are different.

Choose the Best Method

Once a goal is set there is never only one simple way to accomplish it. Before making a strategy decision, it is advisable to think through as many alternative ways of accomplishing the goal as possible, then choose the one that appears to be the best.

As you are making the choice, keep in mind that often the best way to go from A to B is first go to C. My friend, Paul Yonggi Cho, pastor of the world's largest church—the Yoido Full Gospel Church of Seoul, Korea, tells the story of how he obtained the prestigious piece of real estate on Yoido Island in Seoul for his sanctuary. The long-range municipal planning for Yoido Island had designated a church site near the national congress building. Pastor Cho went to the city planner and requested this site for his church, but he was turned down. He was not able to go from A to B.

Cho then inquired who the planner's boss was and found it was the vice-mayor of Seoul. He was not a Christian, but his mother was. So Cho ministered to his mother and she joined his church. Together they led the daughter-in-law, the vice-mayor's wife, to Christ and she joined the church.

Then, through the vice-mayor's wife, Cho was able to talk to the vice-mayor and lead him to Christ. He joined the church and he himself suggested they build a new sanctuary on the Yoido Island property. Cho agreed, and the vice-mayor so instructed his employee, the city planner. To get from A to B, Pastor Cho had to go through C, D and E, but he accomplished the goal.[3]

Does the End Justify the Means?

Clearly, the chief criterion that determines which strategy we choose is whether it accomplishes the goal. This is another way of saying that the end justifies the means. In a broad sense, no other criterion justifies choosing the means you use to accomplish a certain goal. It would be irresponsible to invest time, energy and money in some process that would not achieve your objectives.

Why, then, do ethicists teach that the end does *not* justify the means? Because they are introducing the dimension of morality. If, for example, one effective strategy for making money would be to steal it, the end cannot justify the means because it is an immoral means.

Even a noble goal such as evangelism cannot justify immoral means for doing it. For example, I recently read a newspaper article on a cult called the Children of God (now called "Family of Love"), led by David Berg, which uses sexual contact as an evangelistic methodology. They say that people's sexual appetite is so strong that they have to satisfy it "to prove to them that we really care and we're concerned and that we love them." Here is a clear case of the end *not* justifying the means because the means is immoral.

No, when I assert that the end justifies the means in strategy planning, I am referring to value-neutral means only, not to immoral means. Above all, as I have said, God's work must be done in God's way.

Christian Pragmatism?

Due largely to a fear that immoral means might creep into Christian strategy, we face the widespread attitude that Christians cannot and should not be pragmatic. If pragmatic implies an "anything goes" attitude which may harm others or offend God, I would agree. But I see the term in a different light. My dictionary defines pragmatic as "concerned with practical consequences or values."

I believe that God is genuinely concerned with the practical implementation of His great commission. He wants us to find the lost and bring them back into the fold in the most effective and efficient way possible. He wants us to choose the means which will best accomplish these ends (applying the safeguards I have mentioned above), and this is another way of saying He wants us to be pragmatic.

Uncompromising Principles

I like to call this approach "consecrated pragmatism." While the Church Growth Movement has come in for its share of criticism for being pragmatic, I believe the critics are not understanding it properly as *consecrated* pragmatism. I like the way that Donald McGavran, founder of the Church Growth Movement, puts it. He affirms, as I have done, that doctrinal and ethical principles revealed in the Word of God must never be compromised.

Flexible Methods

McGavran's attitude toward methods is different. He says, "We devise mission methods and policies in the light of what God has blessed—and what He has obviously not blessed." Many methods in current use, he points out, are supposed to bring people to Christ, but they don't. They are supposed to multiply churches, but they don't. They are supposed to improve society, but they don't. "If it does not work to the glory of God and the extension of Christ's church, throw it away and get something which does," McGavran says. "As to methods, we are fiercely pragmatic."[4]

Biblical Precedents

There are several biblical precedents for planning strategies by using consecrated pragmatism. Moses' goal was to judge the people of Israel. He was using the wrong method in doing it by himself. It was not morally wrong, he was simply burning himself out. His father-in-law, Jethro, came up with a pragmatic solution: appoint rulers of thousands, rulers of hundreds, rulers of fifties and rulers of tens. Moses did it and God blessed them (see Exodus 18). The book of Proverbs has numerous passages which refer to wise, pragmatic strategy planning. Here are just a few from *The Living Bible:*

- "We should make plans—counting on God to direct us" (Prov. 16:9).
- "A wise man thinks ahead; a fool doesn't, and even brags about it!" (Prov. 13:16).
- "It is pleasant to see plans develop. That is why fools refuse to give them up even when

they are wrong" (Prov. 13:19).
- "The intelligent man is always open to new ideas. In fact, he looks for them" (Prov. 18:15).

But biblical examples are not limited to the Old Testament. The Apostle Paul was specifically pragmatic in his choice of evangelistic methodologies, and he even flirted with what some of the more rigid theologians of his day might have considered ethical issues. He said that when he was evangelizing Jews, he kept the Jewish law, but he relaxed it when he was evangelizing Gentiles who were not under the law. How does Paul express it? "I have become all things to all men, that I might by all means save some" (1 Cor. 9:22).

Paul did not see this means as immorality or living on a double standard, but rather as part of his servanthood. "I have made myself a servant to all, that I might win the more" (1 Cor. 9:19). And although he himself might have been somewhat uncomfortable, especially with his strategy for reaching the Gentiles, he affirms, "This I do for the gospel's sake" (1 Cor. 9:23).

Historical Precedent

In some recent research on John Wesley's application of church growth principles, George G. Hunter III points out that Wesley's view of pragmatism was much like that of the Apostle Paul. He affirms that Wesley "was an unapologetic pragmatist in the choice and development of strategies, models and methods." Wesley, for example, didn't want to preach in the fields, but he did because it was the best way to evangelize. He summed his attitude up by saying, "I would observe every punctilio or order, except when the salvation of souls is at stake. Then I prefer the end to the means."[5]

————— **Advantages of Having a Strategy** —————

If we accept the biblical pattern of consecrated pragmatism in our thinking about strategy planning, we will find that several advantages accrue:

1. *It increases efficiency.* In order to accomplish any task, an investment of time, energy and money is necessary in some proportion or other. A clearly planned strategy allows us to see what these proportions are and how they are being used toward the goal. Not only does a strategy help us decide what to do, it helps us decide what *not* to do, and that is equally important. A great amount of God's resources go to waste because Christian leaders are majoring on the minors.

2. *It helps measure effectiveness.* A given task is effective when it fulfills its objectives. If the goals and objectives are not clear, there is no way of knowing if a given activity turns out to be effective or not. Strategy planning requires the goals to be clarified, and that enables us to measure our progress and to know if and when we have done what we were supposed to do.

3. *It permits midcourse corrections.* If what we are doing is not working, the sooner we find out about it the better. A well-planned strategy will contain a number of check points where we reassess the methodology we are using. Sometimes only a slight adjustment is necessary, sometimes the procedures will have to be scrapped and a new one substituted.

All too frequently, church and denominational programs are adopted and they continue to be used whether or not they are moving steadily toward the goal. I heard of

one pastor who thought that the best evangelistic methodology was knocking on doors house-by-house, street-by-
street. One year he and his team knocked on 4,000 doors.
"How many converts did you get?" he was asked.

"None," was the reply.

"What are you going to do now?" inquired his friend.

The answer: "We're going to redouble our efforts and
call on 8,000 homes this next year!"

The program was supreme, even though it was producing no results.

4. *It unites the team.* Most often strategies for evangelism and mission involve the participation of more than
one person. Teams, some large and some small, are the
units God usually blesses for outreach and church growth.
When the strategy is adequately planned, each member of
the team understands what contribution he or she is
expected to make toward the task.

Furthermore, each one understands what the other
members of the team are doing as well. Few things are
more frustrating than working with others on a project
when overall coordination and sense of individual and collective responsibility for the outcome is lacking. Good
strategy avoids such frustration.

5. *It makes accountability natural.* Much of God's
work is voluntary. Since people are not being paid for what
they are doing, correcting them is not easy, even when
they need it. Volunteers may accuse us of picking on them
if they are told that they are wrong or inefficient. A clearly
articulated strategy avoids this potential difficulty because
a strategy is a sort of contract binding together the persons who will be implementing it. It is understood from the
outset that each person will be held accountable for the
role they play in accomplishing the task.

6. *It helps others.* While strategies always have to be

adapted to each new situation, when a given strategy is successful it often becomes a model. Others who desire to undertake similar tasks can learn much from a good strategy and use it as a guide rather than starting to develop their own from scratch.

NOTES

1. Anonymous, "The Dilemma of the Reformed Missionary Today," *Reformation Today*, Sussex, England, May-June 1974, p. 21.
2. For further details on how the spiritual gifts operate in the body of Christ specifically for evangelism and church growth, see my book, *Your Spiritual Gifts Can Help Your Church Grow* (Ventura, CA: Regal Books, 1979).
3. Paul Yonggi Cho, *The Fourth Dimension* (Plainfield, NJ: Logos, 1979).
4. C. Peter Wagner, "Pragmatic Strategy for Tomorrow's Mission," *God, Man and Church Growth*, Alan R. Tippett, ed. (Grand Rapids: Wm. B. Eerdmans Publishing Co., 1973), pp. 146-147.
5. George G. Hunter III, "Rediscovering Wesley, The Church Growth Strategist," *Global Church Growth*, January-March 1986, p. 4.

2
Why Aim for Church Growth?

If planning strategy is both biblical and practical, an immediate question arises: What shall we plan a strategy *for?* Every strategy must have a goal, so what should our goal be?

Answers to this question can be as broad as the whole spectrum of Christian activities and ministries. Strategies need to be developed for intensifying our prayer life, for meaningful worship and praise of God, for sharing our material goods with the poor, for a more adequate enjoyment of *koinonia* or fellowship in our churches, for raising funds for a church building program or for organizing a board of deacons. Each one of these (and many other Christian undertakings could be added to the list) requires an individualized treatment. Much could be written about the special characteristics of each ministry.

Here, however, we focus on strategies for church growth. Why? Because, if we concentrate on church growth we get to the heart of the Great Commission. I realize this is a rather categorical statement and may not be accepted at face value by all. Therefore, it will be helpful to discuss some biblical reasons why I believe the best way to go about evangelism and missions is to aim for church growth.

————————— **Church Growth Theology** —————————

Some have criticized the Church Growth Movement for not having a strong enough theological foundation. It has been called "atheological" or "thin on exegetical material." While there seems to be far less of this criticism today than, say, 10 or 15 years ago, we still hear it from time to time.

Donald McGavran, the founder of the Church Growth Movement, sees church growth as *essentially* theological. He never tires of affirming that "God wants His lost sheep found and brought into the fold." This, of course, is a strongly theological assumption held by all advocates of church growth.

A Developing Theology

The critics, however, are asking for more. They want systematically-developed, heavily-footnoted treatises which relate church growth teaching to the classical theological issues raised by the classical Christian theologians. Such scholarship is coming.

Eddie Gibbs's *I Believe in Church Growth*[1] has a substantial theological section. Donald McGavran and Arthur Glasser's *Contemporary Theologies of Mission*[2] relates particularly to the missiological dimensions of church growth theology. My book *Church Growth and the Whole Gospel*[3] attempts to deal with theological issues related to aspects of social ethics impacted by the Church Growth Movement. Some of the newer contributions, such as Ebbie Smith's *Balanced Church Growth*[4] and Kent Hunter's *Foundations for Church Growth*[5], interact with the theological discussions which have emerged through the earlier years of the Church Growth Movement. Eddie Gibbs is finishing a new, important work on biblical foundations of church growth.

I anticipate that the theological development of church growth theory will accelerate in the years to come. Perhaps some of the critics lack the patience which comes from a historical perspective on how and when theology usually develops. Dynamic movements directly involved in Christian ministry rarely begin with theological formulations. They usually begin with activists who simply assume a set of theological premises and go to work to change the world. Systematized theological work usually is developed from a movement, not vice versa.

For example, Jesus never wrote anything, much less a theology. The book of Romans, the most systematized theological development of Jesus' gospel in the Bible, was written 30 years after the preaching of the gospel began. Luther and Calvin did not systematize the theology of the Reformation until after it had begun. Theologians are still working on the theology of the Reformation 450 years later. Christianity was introduced into the Third World over 100 years ago, but only recently are we seeing the emergence of Third World theologies. The Church Growth Movement is only 30 years old, so that is why I think the best theologizing yet lies ahead.

A Differing Methodology

Another interesting fact, sometimes overlooked by the critics, is that church growth has adopted a theological methodology somewhat different from that of the classical theologians. While there is no difference in accepting the absolute authority of the Bible as the foundation of theology, there is a difference in the cognate disciplines which are brought to bear in interpreting the Bible. Classical theologians lean heavily on philosophy and the philosophical method. Church growth, strongly influenced by missiology, leans heavily on the social sciences and the social scientific method. This latter approach develops a theological paradigm which seems so unusual to many traditional theologians that they doubt whether the result is good theology at all.

Take, for instance, the role of Christian experience in theologizing. The two approaches both attempt to relate their theology to Christian experience, but the method of doing it is different. The classical approach judges the validity of any experience on the basis of previously established theological principles. In contrast, church growth leans toward a phenomenological approach which holds theological conclusions somewhat more tentatively and is open to revise them when necessary in the light of what is learned through experience. It is open to the possibility that theological expressions might vary from culture to culture and yet all be faithful to the Word of God.

Differing attitudes towards speaking in tongues illustrate what I am saying. Some theologians, taking the philosophical approach, have decided that speaking in tongues ceased with the apostolic church. Their theology, then, requires them to explain the phenomenon of tongues speaking among Christians today as something other than a bona fide work of the Holy Spirit. Others, taking the phenomenological approach, carefully examine the actual phenomenon of speaking in tongues to discern whether it can be judged to be of the Holy Spirit. If they decide that it is, as many have, they are then willing to reexamine the Scriptures in the light of the experience, and to revise their theology accordingly.

Some become nervous about this because it seems to make theology too relative. But, after all, what is theology? Theology is a human attempt to explain God's Word and works in a reasonable and systematic way. Only the Bible is infallible because it is the Word of God. Theology does not have that quality, as most theologians readily admit. Many of them debate with each other, all arguing that their theology is more biblical than the others, but they stop short of claiming divine inspiration.

—————— Theological Nonnegotiables ——————

All this is not to say that church growth leaders lack strong theological convictions. While I have no right to speak for all those who associate themselves with the Church Growth Movement, I do believe that I represent a large number of them in claiming seven theological nonnegotiables as bedrock for church growth teaching and practice. These assumptions have guided most advocates of church growth for the past 30 years, even though they may not have been as explicit as I am here.

1. *The glory of God is the chief end of humans.* I agree with the famous Westminster Confession in putting God's glory at the top of the list of theological tenets. "Whether you eat or drink, or whatever you do, do all to the glory of God" (1 Cor. 10:31).

2. *Jesus Christ is Lord.* He is the creator and absolute ruler of the universe. "Every tongue should confess that Jesus Christ is Lord, to the glory of God the Father" (Phil. 2:11). This means that we, His servants, must obey His every commandment.

3. *The preaching of the gospel is the preaching of the Kingdom of God.* John the Baptist preached it (see Matt. 3:1-2), Jesus preached it (see Matt. 6:33), the Twelve

preached it (see Matt. 10:7), and Paul preached it (see
Acts 28:30-31). All this indicates that we should preach
the Kingdom of God. We should be clear that the Kingdom
is not some human utopian society on earth, nor is it the
institutional church. The Kingdom is the company of those
who have truly pledged allegiance to the King, almost all of
whom reflect this by being responsible members of Christian churches.

4. *The Scriptures are the only normative authority for
believers.* Church growth people hold a high view of biblical
inspiration. "All Scripture is given by inspiration of God,
... that the man of God may be complete, thoroughly
equipped for every good work" (2 Tim. 3:16-17).

5. *Sin, salvation and eternal death are eschatological
realities.* "For all have sinned and fall short of the glory of
God" (Rom. 3:23) and "the wages of sin is death" (Rom.
6:23). Crucial decisions made in this life influence where a
person will spend eternity.

6. *God wills all to be saved from sin and eternal death.*
His very nature is love and He wants all people reconciled
to Him. For that reason He sent His only son, Jesus
Christ. "The Lord is . . . not willing that any should perish
but that all should come to repentance" (2 Pet. 3:9). As
McGavran would say, "God wants His lost sheep found."

7. *God has given His people a responsibility for saving
souls, and the Holy Spirit works through them to accomplish
the task.* I previously discussed how the divine and human
aspects come together in spreading the gospel. Jesus said,
"You shall receive power when the Holy Spirit has come
upon you; and you shall be witnesses to Me" (Acts 1:8).

———— Jesus' Attitudes Toward Growth ————

In some circles it is popular to say that Jesus was not interested in church growth. Jesus supposedly would hold to the philosophy that small is beautiful. He was not concerned about success, but about faithfulness. The cross brought out His quality of suffering reproach. He was scorned by the society of His day. He called just a few to follow Him. He was interested in quality, not quantity.

Those who see Jesus and His ministry in this light are frequently repulsed by church growth teaching. The enthusiasm and optimism of the Church Growth Movement appears to them to be a sort of unchristian "triumphalism" or even "numerolatry," the worship of numbers for numbers' sake. Because these opinions are somewhat widespread in our day, it is important to examine Jesus' attitudes toward church growth in some detail.

While triumphalism can easily become obnoxious and self-seeking, there is a way of observing a silver lining of triumphalism in the way Jesus looked at His own ministry and mission.

Consider that Jesus had spent three years training a band of disciples. He was coming to the end of His earthly ministry when He would be captured, tried, defamed, spat upon, beaten, stripped naked, mocked and crucified between two thieves. The people of Jerusalem whom He had loved and wept over would form an angry mob and demand His execution. Worse yet, He would be deserted by His closest followers, the very ones He was training to carry on His ministry when He left.

Yet at a time like this when most people would be devastated, Jesus was optimistic. To Him the process He was passing through was not going to end in defeat, but triumph. In the midst of it all He made an audacious prediction: "This gospel of the kingdom will be preached in all the world as a witness to all the nations, and then the end will come" (Matt. 24:14). Up to that point the preaching of the gospel had been pretty well limited to one relatively small people group on the eastern shores of the Mediterranean: Aramaic-speaking Galilean Jews. But Jesus was able to look beyond the immediate circumstances and see the spread of the Kingdom to all the peoples of the earth.

The disciples were discouraged and confused. When the heat came, most of them deserted Jesus. Even after the Resurrection they were unsure of the future, knowing that Jesus would again leave them. True, Jesus had promised to send them the Holy Spirit as their comforter, but the disciples did not yet know what that would mean. In that frame of mind they could scarcely grasp the world-changing implications of the Great Commission which Jesus left with them: "Go therefore and make disciples of all the nations" (Matt. 28:19). They were not sure at that point whether they would be able to make another disciple in Jerusalem, let alone throughout the world. But Jesus wanted them to believe that they could triumph.

Of course, they would endure episodes of trials and persecutions. They would learn how to deal with sufferings and setbacks. But these are seen as mere potholes in the road to world evangelization. Even though tough times would come, and some disciples eventually would give their physical lives, the vision that Jesus gave them of ultimate victory sustained them through it all.

Using Numbers

Not only did Jesus teach the final triumph of the Kingdom of God over the kingdom of darkness, but He also made free use of numbers. I share the concern of some that using numbers can become "numerolatry." Numbers can be used for an ego trip. They can be a manifestation of carnality and draw the focus of glory from God to humans. They can be a tool of the enemy as we read in 1 Chronicles 21:1, "Now Satan stood up against Israel, and moved David to number Israel."

But while there can be danger in using numbers, there can also be blessing to the work of God. It was God, not Satan, who told Moses to count the people of Israel. This is described in a Bible book which carries the very title *Numbers.* "Now the Lord spoke to Moses . . . 'Take a census of all the congregation of the children of Israel'" (Num. 1:1-2). Using numbers is not intrinsically right or wrong. It depends on the motive. David's motive was self-seeking while Moses' motive was to bring good to God's people.

Numbers and Sheep

On many occasions during His ministry Jesus spoke of numbers to teach important truths. Jesus spoke of sheep. I have heard some say, "Jesus told Peter to feed the sheep, not count them." It is true that sheep need to be fed, but that is not all there is to shepherding. Jesus said, "If a man has a hundred sheep, and one of them goes astray, does he not leave the ninety-nine and go to the mountains to seek the one that is straying?" (Matt. 18:12). While Jesus did not explicitly mention counting at this point, it certainly was implicit. As anyone who knows something about sheep farming will attest, the only way for a farmer with 100 sheep to know how many are in the sheepfold is to count them.

Jesus was using sheep as a metaphor for people. Some people are safe in God's fold, and some are lost. In America today, at the very most, 70 are in the fold and 30 lost, but more realistically only 40 may be in the fold and 60 lost. Worldwide, we have 30 in the fold at most and 70 lost.

What is Jesus saying to us? He is not saying "small is beautiful" and we should be satisfied with the few sheep which happen to be in the fold. No, He is telling us to get our eyes on the lost and seek them until they are found. God does not want just a few sheep, He wants many. "It is not the will of your Father who is in heaven that one of these little ones should perish" (Matt. 18:14).

Numbers and Grain

Jesus spoke of grain. He knew that it is very important to a farmer whether the yield is 30, 60, or 100 times the number of seeds planted. A small grain harvest is never characterized as "beautiful." That is why Jesus desires the largest possible labor force for harvesting. He said, "Pray the Lord of the harvest to send out laborers into His harvest" (Matt. 9:38).

Numbers and Fish

Jesus spoke of fish. He realized that it is important for fishers to count their catch. It is recorded that when Jesus helped His disciples fish in the Sea of Tiberias they pulled in 153 large fish (see John 21:11). Presumably that was better than if they had pulled in 19 or 64 or even 152. And Jesus said, "I will make you fishers of men" (Matt. 4:19). It is better to win 153 persons to Jesus Christ than 152. The more fish the better!

God Himself has no aversion to counting and keeping records. Jesus said that God keeps records of how many sparrows there are, and even how many hairs each one of us has on our head (see Luke 12:6-7). The spread of the

Kingdom of God is supposed to be like a mustard plant which begins as a small seed, but grows into a large tree (see Matt. 13:31-32). Growth is an inherent quality of our task of spreading the good news of Jesus Christ, and not something we should apologize for.

Richard B. Wilkie, the prominent United Methodist bishop, strongly urges his fellow Methodists to get back to the proper use of numbers. In a remarkable book, *And Are We Yet Alive?* he responds to those who, in recent years, have been saying, "I don't believe in the numbers game." He is understandably concerned that his denomination has lost some 2 million members in the past two decades. He laments that, so far as meaningful statistics are concerned, Methodists have been walking in the dark. "Ignorance of statistics," Wilkie says, "is ultimately a cheap cop-out for not caring whether an organization lives or dies. Statistics represent people," he argues, " . . . and any enterprise that ignores essential data travels the road to oblivion."[6]

The Results of Jesus' Ministry

Jesus ministered for three years, then was crucified. What were the concrete results of three years of work? It is important that we first see the meaning of the cross, then look at both the quantity and the quality of the disciples which Jesus made.

Success-oriented

Some have argued that ending up on a cross proves that Jesus was not success-oriented. The cross is made out to reflect mere faithfulness at best and failure at worst. But I do not see the cross as a symbol of failure, I see it rather as a complete success.

As Jesus was explaining His need to go to the cross, He said, "Unless a grain of wheat falls into the ground and dies, it remains alone; but if it dies, it produces much grain" (John 12:24). He came to save people from their sins, and He could not have done it except for the cross. Jesus rejected the idea of asking His Father to save Him from this hour. He said, rather, "For this purpose I came to this hour" (John 12:27). Then, "I, if I am lifted up from the earth, will draw all peoples to Myself" (John 12:32).

Good Quantity

The cross was a means toward an end. And, although Jesus dreaded it, as we observe in Gethsemane (see Matt. 26:37-39), He was pragmatic enough to do what was necessary to succeed. His death on the cross did open the way of salvation to increasing multitudes. In church growth terms, what did Jesus accomplish? Some assume that Jesus saw very slow growth and that only a few responded. But on the measuring scales which we now use, He did very well. If a church planter goes into a pioneer territory and the work grows to at least 500, possibly 650, in just three years, that is considered successful. No bishop or district superintendent would complain. Jesus left 120 faithful followers in Jerusalem, and over 500 in Galilee—whether they included the 120 we do not know.

High Quality

So the quantity was good, but how about the quality? From the information we have, it was a high quality Christian group and probably comparable to the members of a good Christian church today. We possibly know more about Peter than any of the others. Peter was one of the select Twelve, and one of the elite inner three. Most of us consider him a fairly good Christian. Yet, after three years in the personal company of the Messiah, he denied Jesus three times, he wouldn't—without persuasion—tell Jesus he loved Him completely, he went back to fishing as soon as Jesus was gone and even after Pentecost he was somewhat racist and had to be scolded by Paul.

Even though the group Jesus left behind were not all Mother Theresas or George Müellers they were good people who wanted to serve Jesus and who formed a solid base for the subsequent expansion of the Christian movement throughout the Roman Empire. From the church growth perspective, I would say that Jesus was successful.

Continuing Growth in Acts

If the ministry of Jesus was successful, the ministry of the apostles after Pentecost was even more so. Their experiences, recorded in the book of Acts, span a 30-year period. In those 30 years, the original 500 or so grew to several tens of thousands, with some estimates as high as 100,000 in Palestine alone.

Goal-oriented

For a study of strategy, it is important to notice that Acts is a goal-oriented book. The goal statement is found in the first chapter: "You shall receive power when the Holy Spirit has come upon you; and you shall be witnesses to Me in Jerusalem, and in all Judea and Samaria, and to the end of the earth" (Acts 1:8). The following narrative reflects the attitude of a people, neither intimidated by triumphalism nor advocating that "small is beautiful."

Rather, we find an attitude of rejoicing when 3,000 came to faith in Jesus Christ the first day of the evangelistic effort. What we see is a group of people saying to each other, "The Lord has given us a task to accomplish—let's get on with it."

People-oriented

Because Jesus' goal is to reach people, we find that Acts is also a people-oriented book. As I will develop in detail later on, contemporary evangelistic and missionary strategy is being formulated around the "people approach to world evangelization." The book of Acts describes the spread of the gospel from what we today call "people group" to "people group." The first believers were Galilean Jews. Then the gospel jumped to Hellenistic Jews in Jerusalem, then to Hebrews in Judea, then to Samaritans, then to an African, then to other Gentiles.

Results-oriented

Acts is also a results-oriented book. The statement, "Our task is to preach the gospel and leave the results to God," contains enough truth to make it deceiving. While it is true that "God . . . gives the increase" (1 Cor. 3:7) we dare not say, "We must not be concerned about the results of our evangelistic efforts." Since we are God's instruments for world evangelization, if God is concerned about results we must be concerned also.

The book of Acts provides a model. "That day about three thousand souls were added to them" (Acts 2:41). "Many of those who heard the word believed; and the number of the men came to be about five thousand" (Acts 4:4). "And some of them were persuaded; and a great

multitude of the devout Greeks, and not a few of the leading women, joined Paul and Silas" (Acts 17:4). And on and
on.

Those are some of the successes, but in strategy evaluation it is also essential to know of the failures. The book
of Acts records many. Paul in Athens, for example, saw
only a sparse harvest. "Some mocked, while others said,
'We will hear you again on this matter'" (Acts 17:32).
After fervently testifying to King Agrippa, Paul heard his
disappointing words, "You almost persuade me to become
a Christian" (Acts 26:28), but "almost" was not good
enough. When we do not accomplish our goal, it is helpful
to know it so we can revise our strategy where it has been
weak.

——— A Closer Look at the Great Commission ———

The Great Commission of Jesus, I repeat, is at the core of
planning strategy for evangelism and missions. It is the
key commandment for the Church Growth Movement.
Church growth leaders believe that Jesus is Lord and that
all of His commandments must be obeyed by faithful Christians. However, obeying this particular commandment—
without detracting from the others—is the specialization
of the Church Growth Movement.

The Commandment

That we fully understand the meaning of the Great Commission then is essential before we begin planning strategy. Above all, we must make sure we understand the
true goal of the Great Commission. If we are aiming at the
wrong goal, all our subsequent strategy planning will be in
vain.

The Great Commission appears five times: in Matthew, Mark, Luke, John and Acts. Of the five, the most basic text for understanding strategy components is Matthew 28:19-20:

> "Go therefore and make disciples of all the nations, baptizing them in the name of the Father and of the Son and of the Holy Spirit, teaching them to observe all things that I have commanded you."

The Goal

Notice there are four verbs in the Great Commission: "go," "make disciples," "baptize" and "teach." Though not so obvious in English, in the original Greek three of the verbs are participles or helping verbs and only one is imperative—the command verb. The one imperative is *make disciples*. This, then, is the goal of the Great Commission.

The Means

Going, baptizing and teaching are the helping verbs or the means toward the end of making disciples. This is not to say that going, baptizing and teaching are unimportant. Disciples cannot be made without doing these things, so they have somewhat an imperative flavor also. But none of them is the goal of the Great Commission. Making disciples is.

The list of activities that are means toward the end of making disciples is expanded in the other four statements of the Great Commission. In Mark 16:15-16 preaching is added. Luke 24:47-48 adds witnessing. John 20:21-23 adds sending and forgiving sins. Acts 1:8 brings up witnessing again and gives the geographical scope.

Many attempts at planning strategies for evangelism and missions break down at precisely this point. They take only a partial look at the Great Commission and conclude that it is fulfilled by preaching or by witnessing or by sending missionaries. All of these ministries are necessary, but the Great Commission is fulfilled only when disciples are made.

What Is a Disciple?

If making disciples is the goal of the Great Commission, it becomes necessary to make sure we know what a disciple is so we can evaluate whether our strategy has been successful or not.

What a Disciple Is Not

Few would equate disciples with persons who raise their hands at an evangelistic crusade or who walk the sawdust trail or even who pray the sinner's prayer. Experience shows that many who do these things do not continue on as followers of Jesus. But some evangelistic strategies seem satisfied with these responses even so. I will discuss this later, but note here that disciples are something more than persons who express an interest in the gospel.

Some err on the other extreme by loading too much meaning on the biblical concept of disciple. To them a disciple is a well-polished Christian, exemplary in every way. After you become a Christian, according to this point of view, you then go through a process which leads you finally to become a disciple.

What a Disciple Is

The biblical meaning of disciple is somewhere between these two extremes. The word "disciple" (*mathetes* in Greek) is equivalent to "Christian." The *Interpreter's Dictionary of the Bible* says, "'Disciple' is the most frequent and general term for believers in Christ."[7] *The New Bible Dictionary* says, "The most common use of *mathetes* was in denoting adherents of Jesus . . . believers, those who confess Jesus as the Christ."[8] Most other Bible scholars whom I have consulted agree.

So what is a disciple? A Christian. Disciples are people who have been born again by the Spirit of God. They have confessed with their mouths the Lord Jesus and believed in their hearts that God has raised Him from the dead (see Rom. 10:9-10). Disciples are new creatures in Christ Jesus. They may have their ups and downs, but they are part of the family of God. Peter was a disciple even in those dark days when he was denying his Lord. Joseph of Arimathaea was a disciple, even though he kept it a secret. But in general the life of a disciple is characterized by continuing "steadfastly in the apostles' doctrine and fellowship, in the breaking of bread, and in prayers" (Acts 2:42).

What Discipling Is

I realize that today many say, "I am in the discipling ministry," meaning that they nurture other Christians. I understand this language, and am not suggesting it should be changed. But those who use it in this sense need to recognize that this concept of "making disciples" is not what is referred to in the Great Commission. The raw material of making disciples in the Great Commission sense is *unbe-*

lievers who need to commit their lives to Christ for the first time. The raw material of modern "disciple making" is *Christians* who need to be helped along the continuing road of Christian discipleship.

The word "disciple" appears about 260 times in the New Testament. All of these appearances are in the Gospels and Acts, the books on the establishment and growth of the Christian movement. Not even once does the word "disciple" appear in the Epistles, the books of Christian nurture. I stress this so that those called to planning a strategy to fulfill the Great Commission will not be confused as to the goal. It is to bring men and women over the borderline from the kingdom of darkness to the kingdom of light. The subsequent instruction follows once the person has become a disciple.

But, some will say, doesn't the Great Commission say "teaching them to observe all things"? It does, but this must be understood in the correct context. In the original Greek the object of the verb "teaching" can be understood either as the "all things" or the "to observe." I agree with the scholars who argue that the "to observe" is the correct interpretation. This means that in order to become a disciple one has to agree to obey Jesus from that point on. It means that Jesus is Lord as well as Saviour. After that the Christian spends a lifetime discovering more and more what the "all things" includes.[9]

─────── **The Fruit of Becoming a Disciple** ───────

The above, I believe, is good theory, but how does it work out in practice? If knowing whether or not people are becoming disciples is necessary to test the validity of a chosen strategy, how can we be sure when we have one that is valid?

Theological Validity

From the purely theological perspective, a disciple is made when the power of the Holy Spirit comes and makes that person a new creature. "Therefore, if anyone is in Christ, he is a new creation; old things have passed away; behold, all things have become new" (2 Cor. 5:17). This is salvation. The new birth. The moment at which one's name is written in the Lamb's Book of Life.

But while theologically this is valid, strategically it is not very helpful. I cannot look anyone's name up in the Lamb's Book of Life. The transformation in the person's life is invisible. So how do I know whether it has really happened?

Jesus said, "By their fruits you will know them" (Matt. 7:20). The life of a true Christian should be characterized by many fruits. Several of them might constitute valid tests as to whether or not a person is a disciple.

Strategical Validity

But the test used through the years by the Church Growth Movement is responsible church membership. A person's commitment to Christ may be invisible, but the same person's commitment to the Body of Christ is visible and measurable. The two commitments should not be separated. If a person who professes to be a Christian is not a responsible church member, I need at least to raise questions about the validity of the profession.

By this assertion, I do not mean that church membership saves anyone. Only faith in Jesus Christ can save. But strategically speaking, we need to measure the outcome of our activities in some way, and responsible church membership is a reasonable measurement.

This is what I meant when I said earlier that, if we concentrate on church growth, we get to the heart of the Great Commission. The more we evangelize and the more disciples we make, the more churches will be multiplied and grow. And this is why, in planning strategies, we aim for church growth.

NOTES

1. Eddie Gibbs, *I Believe in Church Growth* (Grand Rapids: Wm. B. Eerdmans Publishing Co., 1982).
2. Arthur F. Glasser and Donald A. McGavran, *Contemporary Theologies of Mission* (Grand Rapids: Baker Book House, 1983).
3. C. Peter Wagner, *Church Growth and the Whole Gospel: A Biblical Mandate* (New York: Harper & Row, Publishers Inc., 1981).
4. Ebbie C. Smith, *Balanced Church Growth* (Nashville: Broadman Press, 1984).
5. Kent R. Hunter, *Foundations of Church Growth* (New Haven, MO: Leader, 1983).
6. Richard B. Wilkie, *And Are We Yet Alive?* (Nashville: Abingdon Press, 1986), p. 50.
7. Pierson Parker, "Disciple," *Interpreter's Dictionary of the Bible*, vol. 1 (New York: Abingdon Press, 1962).
8. J.D. Douglas, "Disciple," *The New Bible Dictionary*, J.D. Douglas, ed. (Grand Rapids: Wm. B. Eerdmans Publishing Co., 1962).
9. For a full discussion of this point from the point of view of New Testament exegesis, see Dennis Oliver, *Make Disciples*, D.Miss. dissertation (Pasadena: Fuller Seminary School of World Mission, 1973).

3

The Harvest Principle

In his classic textbook, *Understanding Church Growth,* Donald A. McGavran wrote a section on "Search Theology and a Theology of Harvest."[1] With that he introduced a vocabulary which has persisted among church growth advocates through the years. Using the biblical metaphor of the harvest and all that goes into producing a harvest has proved to be a very helpful way to conceptualize what the growth of the church is all about.

"Search theology" means that our goal in evangelism and mission is to go to the lost, help them in every way possible and, in most cases, make known to them the gospel message. Whether or not they actually become followers of Jesus Christ is inconsequential. In fact many search theologians feel that it might be offensive to push one's religious beliefs on others. They are the type who insist that the results of our outreach efforts should not be counted. God, they say, keeps the records and knows the results, so we should leave that to Him.

McGavran strongly repudiates a theology of search as "out of harmony with the mainstream of Christian revelation." He says that an attitude of simply searching without a deep wish to convert "is not biblically justified." The apostles and the early Church would have repudiated it. "Mere search is not what God wants," says McGavran, "God wants His lost children found."[2]

The other side is a "theology of harvest." Church growth advocates have followed McGavran's lead in stressing the principle of the harvest as a launching pad for planning strategies of church growth. It is such an important concept that it needs to be discussed in detail, and its implications for evangelism and missions clearly drawn out.

The Principle of the Harvest

The world of Jesus' day was an agriculturally oriented world. While there were some large cities in the Roman Empire, most citizens were rural people. Even many who lived in the towns and villages and small cities kept garden plots outside the city walls. They knew what it was to work the soil. This is why Jesus used so much agricultural language in His preaching and teaching. He did not have to explain the implications to His hearers.

Today's world, especially in the industrialized nations, is quite different. Many urban people have had no experience on the farm. If they have any experience with the soil at all, it is as a hobbyist rather than a professional. It is necessary, therefore, to explain some of Jesus' agricultural metaphors from the perspective of a farmer if their implications are going to be helpful for planning strategy.

The Principle

The most fundamental principle of farming is that of the harvest. It is the vision of the fruit. The goal of the strategy which the farmer plans is that of gathering in a crop of whatever is planted. Jesus assumed this when He spoke to His disciples about the harvest: "Lift up your eyes and look at the fields, for they are already white for the harvest! (John 4:35). He mentioned that in some cases one person sows the seed while another gathers the fruit, but they rejoice together because their combined labors have resulted in a harvest (see John 4:36-37).

The Criterion

Farming is enjoyable. I come from a farming background and believe it is one of the most rewarding professions. But enjoyable as farming might be, professional farmers evaluate everything they do on whether a given activity contributes to the harvest. They prepare the ground and sow the seed not as an enjoyable end in itself, but as a step toward the harvest. They dig out weeds and build fences as protection against predators in order to increase the harvest. They walk through their fields in such a way as not to jeopardize the harvest. Then, when the crop is mature, they gather it in with great care in order to maximize the yield.

The Means

If Christian leaders today would look at their task of reaching the world for Jesus Christ with the intensity that a farmer considers the harvest, it would make a measurable difference in the effectiveness of planning strategy. It relates directly to what I spoke of before as consecrated pragmatism. If the end is the harvest, the means to achieve it will constantly be scrutinized to see if they need adjustment.

Unfortunately, in practical terms, the means we are using for evangelism and missions often become just like ends in themselves. We sometimes preach the gospel for the sake of preaching the gospel. We broadcast on the radio for the sake of producing new programs. We send missionaries because it is a good thing to do. But if we follow the harvest principle, we will evaluate our activities in terms, for example, not of how many missionaries we send, but how many lost people we reach and bring to Jesus Christ. We will never be satisfied with "good" outreach programs that are supposed to bring people to Christ but do not.

_____ **The Principle of Sowing** _____

The Parable

Jesus' parable of the sower (see Matt. 13:1-23) brings out a principle of both agriculture and evangelism that many biblical expositors do not catch. Attempt to interpret Jesus' words as a farmer would. A farmer goes out to sow seed. The seed, a valuable commodity, falls into four places. In only one of the four places does it accomplish its purpose which is to produce fruit. In three of the four places the seed produces no fruit and the farmer is obviously disappointed.

The Interpretation

If a farmer were interpreting the parable, the major question would be: Why? What did the one place that produced fruit have that the other three did not? Could it have been the sower? Perhaps a different person sowed the seed on the fourth place? No, the same person sowed all the seed. Perhaps it was the climate, always an important agricultural variable. But no, climate does not seem to be a factor. How about the seed? Was a special hybrid seed introduced in the fourth place? No, the interpretation of the parable which Jesus gives later on says, "The seed is the word of God" (Luke 8:11). The same seed, the Word of God, fell on all four places.

This brings up an interesting fact that many people have failed to recognize. Apparently, according to the parable, the seed of the Word of God can be sown without producing fruit. Some people resist this idea on the basis of Isaiah 55:11: "So shall My word be that goes forth from My mouth; It shall not return to Me void." They feel that Isaiah gives them a promise that no matter what procedure is used, so long as the Bible is quoted, unbelievers will be saved. I had a friend years ago who would stand on a chair in a crowded restaurant and recite John 3:16 on the hypothesis that it was God's Word and would not return void. No, I see Isaiah 55 as a poetic expression of the sovereignty of God, not as a fail-safe formula to justify any given evangelistic methodology.

In fact, to take the thought one step further, careless use of the Word of God can even serve the purposes of the enemy. In the parable, Jesus says that the seed which fell along the roadway was eaten by the birds. Then in the interpretation he likens the birds to the wicked one. No farmer wants precious seed to be used as bird feed. No evangelist wants the Word of God to be given out only to be snatched away by the devil.

The Application

How can this be avoided? The parable says that the seed

which fell on good ground produced fruit thirty-, sixty- and one hundredfold. The fertility of the soil, then, is the most important independent variable. This "soil," according to the interpretation, is people who have been so prepared that they hear the word and understand it (see Matt. 13:23).

So one way to increase the effectiveness of evangelistic strategy planning is to determine ahead of time which individuals or groups of individuals have hearts prepared by the Holy Spirit to receive the Word. As we know, one of the roles of the Holy Spirit is to "convict the world of sin, and of righteousness, and of judgment" (John 16:8). As he does this, we need to be alert and discerning, moving as much as possible where God is already moving.

Careless broadcast sowing of the gospel message is not usually the most effective evangelistic procedure. To the degree possible, and later on I will share some of the technology available for doing this, we should test the evangelistic soil. Once we test the soil, we can use the energy and time and other resources available for our evangelistic task in a much more productive way. As I have said before, the task of sowing the seed is not an end in itself; it is a means toward the end of producing the fruit.

The Principle of Pruning

In agriculture, pruning refers to removing unnecessary or unproductive branches from a plant. When this is done properly, the resulting harvest is greater. The same principle applies to culling or removing unproductive animals from the flock or the herd. Thinning or removing superfluous plants is also frequently necessary for increasing the amount of fruit.

The Parable

Jesus also had something to say about unproductive plants. His parable of the fig tree describes the principle in graphic terms. "'A certain man had a fig tree planted in his vineyard, and he came seeking fruit on it and found none'" (Luke 13:6). For three years he had expected fruit from the tree, and it had not produced.

So the owner of the tree spoke to a farmhand and told him to cut it down. The hired man, who obviously had an emotional attachment to the tree, objected. He promised to work harder and add fertilizer, if the owner would let the tree grow for one more year. With no resolution to the story, we do not know what finally was decided.

But what I want to highlight is the focus of interest on the part of the two persons. The farmer's interest was the fruit. The worker's interest was the tree. To the farmer the tree was simply a means toward the end of getting figs. If it did not produce, he wanted it removed and the ground used for some other plant that would produce fruit.

The Application

The principle of pruning needs to be applied to our outreach efforts whether they are evangelistic crusades or missionary ventures. All too often we become fascinated by the tree. It grows, it has beautiful green leaves, it provides shade, it is a fine ornament. By the same token, evangelistic programs can produce activity, they can get people excited, they can attract media attention, they can successfully raise funds, and they can absorb a great deal of energy.

In a subtle way, the evangelistic process can become an end in itself; and when it does, the matter of whether or not it produces fruit becomes relatively insignificant. The program is what counts, and it will be defended with considerable emotion if challenged. The result is that frequently large quantities of resources, both human and financial, are frequently used in relatively unproductive evangelistic efforts.

Here is where pragmatism enters the picture once again. Good strategy planning will build in frequent tests to determine whether the expected results are, in fact, taking place. If they are not, emotional ties should not prevent us from scrapping any methodology which is not working, even above the protests of people who, like the hired man, enjoy what they are doing and are indifferent toward the fruit. We must be willing to say, "Cut it down; why does it use up the ground?"

The Principle of Reaping

The harvest is the payoff for the farmer. It is the most crucial time of the agricultural cycle. Jesus said, "The harvest truly is plentiful, but the laborers are few. Therefore pray the Lord of the harvest to send out laborers into His harvest" (Matt. 9:37-38). Jesus specifically stresses the need for large numbers when the harvest is ripe. Farmers of every part of the world know how important this is.

The state of California, where I live, enjoys the largest agricultural production in the U.S.A. In fact, I read a report that one county alone, Fresno County, if it were a nation would rank seventh in world agricultural production. A good bit of California's agricultural economy relies on Mexican farm workers who are organized into a union called United Farm Workers of America (UFW). It is headed by Cesar Chavez. Knowing the principle of reaping, Cesar Chavez calls a strike at only one time during the year—at the harvest. That is the time the lack of workers can ruin the farmers financially.

Not all harvests ripen at the same time, whether in agriculture or in evangelism. Hundreds of families in America make their living by reaping wheat. None of them is in North Dakota in June. There is plenty of wheat in North Dakota at that time, but none is yet ripe for the harvest. The harvesters are down in Texas and Oklahoma where the wheat is ripe.

I often use the analogy of an apple farm. Suppose I have an apple farm with three fields. In the first field the apples are so ripe that one worker can reap five bushels in one hour. In the second field only a few have ripened and it would take five hours just to reap one bushel. In the third are no ripe apples at all. I have 30 workers to send out to pick apples. Where to send them is not a difficult decision. I would not send all 30 into the first field where the apples are ripe, but I would send 29.

I would ask the other worker to go into the second field and pick as many apples as possible, but frequently to travel over to the third field as well. When this worker returns, I do not expect to see a great number of apples. In this case, I am more interested in information than apples. Through this person I will know when the other fields ripen, and on that basis I will redeploy my work force. The harvest is what determines the quantity of workers employed.

A frequent error is made by evangelistic associations, missionary agencies, denominational bureaucracies and local church outreach committees. When they have three fields similar to the ones I have described, they will send out 30 workers equally to all three fields—10-10-10—on the principle of equity. They will apportion their budget in the same way. Sending the workers may even become more important to some than reaping the harvest. For them, opportunity rather than harvest determines the quantity of workers.

As soon as I say this, many will immediately think of the resistant peoples of the world such as Muslims. Does the principle of reaping mean that we should bypass them? Are the missionaries to the resistant peoples out of the will of God? My answer is no to both questions. We do not bypass the resistant, but neither do we pour in workers as if it were a ripened harvest field. As Donald McGavran frequently says, "We hold them lightly." We send workers to them just as I suggested we send a worker into the apple field with very few ripe apples. In such cases we do not judge the performance of the worker by the harvest. I will have some more to say about this shortly.

____ The Harvest Principle in Jesus' Ministry ____

Targeting our primary attention on people who resemble either fertile soil or a ripened harvest field may appeal to those attuned to careful strategy planning. But the biblical texts which have been cited are parables or passages which are rather abstract and thus subject to a variety of possible interpretations. Is there anything more concrete in Scripture which would help us to see the value of the harvest principle?

I believe there is. As I review the methodologies of both Jesus and Paul, I see the application of the harvest principle.

One of the more unfortunate chapter divisions in the New Testament is the division between Matthew 9 and Matthew 10. Jesus' appeal for prayer that God will send forth laborers into the harvest is the very end of Matthew 9. Because of the chapter division, many who read the

Bible do not realize that the first part of chapter 10 details the way Jesus felt the harvesting should be done. He called His laborers together—the 12 apostles—and told them He was going to send them out. He wanted them to preach the Kingdom of heaven. He gave them power to heal the sick and to cast out demons. But notice that He did not send them out to people in general. He was quite specific as to evangelistic targets.

In those days, the three major people groups in the area were Jews, Gentiles and Samaritans. Jesus said, "Do not go into the way of the Gentiles, and do not enter a city of the Samaritans. But go rather to the lost sheep of the house of Israel" (Matt. 10:5-6). By doing this, Jesus was sending His workers into a ripened harvest field.

At that point in time the Samaritans were not ready. Later the harvest ripened, and Philip was the first reaper, along with Peter and John (see Acts 8:4-25). The Gentiles were not ready either. The great Gentile harvest began years later in Antioch as we see in Acts 11:20-26. Eventually Christian workers were sent to Samaritans and Gentiles, but if the 12 apostles had gone there while Jesus was still alive, they would have had little fruit indeed.

During the time of Jesus' ministry, many Jews were receptive to the gospel. But not all were. Jesus prepared His disciples for this when He said, "Now whatever city or town you enter, inquire who in it is worthy, and stay there till you go out" (Matt. 10:11). This is a method of seeking out the receptive. On the other hand, Jesus said that if people would not receive them or hear their words, they were to depart from that house or city and "shake off the dust from your feet" (Matt. 10:14). Shaking off dust was a culturally-recognized sign of protest, in this case protesting resistance to the gospel.

This procedure was just common sense. Jesus' vision

was for the fruit. His resources were limited to 12 people. Only a finite amount of energy could be or would be expended in this evangelistic tour. As a competent strategy planner, Jesus took as many precautions as possible to see that the output of energy resulted in the maximum harvest.

All this is not to deny that there were other factors which entered into Jesus' planning. Covenant theologians, for example, would remind us that there are theological reasons why the gospel should have gone first to the Jews. The whole process leading up to this was complex, and I would not want to oversimplify it. But whatever led up to it, even if the trail goes as far back as Abraham, the fact remains that God had prepared more Jews to listen to the gospel of the Kingdom at that point in time than Samaritans or Gentiles. Jesus knew this and acted on the information.

____ The Harvest Principle in Paul's Ministry ____

It required some trial-and-error experimentation for the Apostle Paul to locate the ripened harvest field as he moved out to plant churches among the Gentiles. But he soon discovered that the Jewish synagogue community was the place where he was most likely to find Gentiles whose hearts had been prepared by the Holy Spirit to receive the gospel. On his first term of service in Salamis "they preached the word of God in the synagogues" (Acts 13:5). In Iconium "they went together to the synagogue of the Jews" (Acts 14:1).

Then on his second term, after a furlough in Antioch, Paul and his group made some false starts in Asia and Bithynia, but were gently guided by the Holy Spirit to Macedonia. Philippi had no synagogue, but on the Sabbath they went to the place "where prayer was customarily made" (Acts 16:13), a functional substitute for the synagogue in places where there were not yet the required 10 adult Jewish males to constitute a synagogue. When they left Philippi they bypassed Amphipolis and Apollonia in order to get to Thessalonica "where there was a synagogue of the Jews" (Acts 17:1). Subsequently they went to synagogues in Berea, Athens and Corinth.

What was going on? How was Paul applying the harvest principle?

Locating the Field

First of all, it must be remembered that Paul was essentially a missionary to the Gentiles. At the time of his conversion on the Damascus Road, Jesus said that He would deliver Paul "from the Gentiles, to whom I now send you" (Acts 26:17). Paul says that "the gospel for the uncircumcised had been committed to me" (Gal. 2:7). True, he said that the gospel was "for the Jew first and also for the Greek" (Rom. 1:16), but he himself became the great apostle to the Gentiles.

Following the Strategy

It does seem somewhat ironic, then, that in order to expedite his mission to convert Gentiles, Paul would go to the Jewish synagogue. Amphipolis and Apollonia, for example, were Gentile cities. As Paul traveled through the area on foot, he undoubtedly stayed overnight at an inn in both of those cities. I would imagine that he witnessed to the innkeepers and to fellow travelers. But he apparently had no intention of developing a nucleus of Gentile believers in order to plant a church in either Amphipolis or Apollonia, because neither one of them had a synagogue of the Jews. Paul knew by then that the most receptive Gentiles were found, strangely enough, in the synagogue community.

The first century synagogue community was composed of three distinct groups of people. At the heart of each synagogue community were the hard-core Jews. They had been born of Jewish parents and circumcised on the eighth day. They could trace their genealogies back to Abraham. They had never eaten pork or shellfish or meat offered to idols. And most of them were so ethnocentric that they believed it was necessary for a Gentile to become a Jew in order to be accepted as a follower of Jehovah God. Spiritually speaking, only Jews could make it.

In almost every synagogue there were also two groups of Gentiles. The first was called "proselytes," because they had bought into the teaching of the Jews and converted. They were attracted to Jehovah God and were willing to pay the price to follow Him. The males were circumcised, they agreed to obey the law and keep the Sabbath, they made pilgrimages to Jerusalem, and from then on they were no longer Gentiles, but Jews.

The second group of Gentiles was called God-fearers. They were also attracted to Jehovah God and the life of the synagogue community. But, probably for a variety of reasons, they did not choose to take the step of cutting ties with their Gentile roots and becoming Jews. But they did attend the synagogue on a regular basis even though they were kept on the periphery and not allowed full participation. It is important to recognize that the proselytes were ex-Gentiles, while the God-fearers were still Gentiles.

When Paul arrived at the synagogue, he was given celebrity treatment because he was a well-known rabbi and probably even had been a member of the Sanhedrin. He was offered the pulpit, and his message turned out to be a new one. While he had something to say to all three groups in the synagogue community, his primary objective was to convert the Gentiles who were there, the God-fearers. The core of his message was that through Jesus the Messiah, Jehovah God was willing to accept Gentiles into His family as Gentiles. They did not have to become Jews. They did not have to be circumcised. They did not have to repudiate their Gentile friends and relatives.

Reaping the Harvest

This was good news to the God-fearers, and they were ready to accept it. Their hearts were open. The Holy Spirit had been at work in preparing the God-fearers as fertile soil. Lydia was an example (see Acts 16:14). Cornelius was another (see Acts 10:1). They heard the Word and understood it, and Paul saw fruit thirty-, sixty- and one-hundredfold.

Of course, the Jews and proselytes became enraged. Paul was preaching exactly the opposite message from theirs. They still wanted to insist that the Gentiles become Jews. A few of them did become followers of Jesus such as the two synagogue presidents in Corinth (see Acts 18:8,17), but the bulk of them rioted and in many cases drove Paul out of town. They drove him out of Antioch, Iconium, Lystra, Thessalonica, Berea, and almost out of Corinth. But not until the nucleus of a growing Gentile church had been established in each place primarily by converted God-fearing Gentiles.

Obeying the Spirit

Some Bible students object to the thought that the Apostle

Paul consciously planned his strategy. They say that Paul did not premeditate his actions, but rather followed the leading of the Holy Spirit for each new step. I see it differently. I believe the Holy Spirit showed Paul that He had prepared the hearts of God-fearers in the Roman Empire and ripened them as a harvest field. Paul simply obeyed the Holy Spirit by locating synagogue communities with some God-fearers and sharing the gospel with them. It is not a matter of either planning strategy or following the Holy Spirit's leading. It is both/and.

"God gave the increase" (1 Cor. 3:6). Our task is to locate the ripened harvest fields and reap them in Jesus' name. This is the harvest principle.

NOTES

1. Donald A. McGavran, *Understanding Church Growth* (Grand Rapids: Wm. B. Eerdmans Publishing Co., 1980), pp. 26-40.
2. Ibid., p. 32.

4
Testing the Soil

The agricultural world regularly deals with a variety of soils. Even on the same farm there might be many different kinds of soil. Farmers who take planning seriously make soil maps of their farms, test the soil in each section and adjust their methodologies to the demands of each particular soil.

The evangelistic world is also characterized by many "soils" which are known as people groups. Every nation and every city is a mosaic of a variety of natural groupings of people. While some of them might be geographically concentrated such as in a Chinatown or a Little Italy or on an Indian reservation, many other people groups are much more scattered, and they network through social rather than geographical webs. In any case, an important step in planning strategies of church growth is to identify the people group in a given area. I am going to deal later with some of the methods used to distinguish one people group from another, but here it is necessary only to recognize that they exist and that they are an important starting point for what we are calling evangelistic soil testing.

The purpose of testing the soil is to determine, as

much as possible, which people groups might be the most receptive to the gospel at any given time. Conversely, it is helpful to know which of them seem to be resistant to the message of the Kingdom. Once this is known, as we saw in the last chapter, intelligent decisions as to how to deploy personnel and allocate resources can be made.

It is important to think through two relevant questions in beginning to consider soil testing: (1) Is it desirable? and (2) Is it possible?

—————— **Is Soil Testing Desirable?** ——————

In the preceding chapter, I attempted as best I could to argue that evangelistic soil testing is desirable. If our goal is fruit, then maximizing yields as related to investments of time, energy and money only makes sense.

But, some will say, such reasoning is worldly. It is applying secular principles to God's work. The Holy Spirit is sovereign and unpredictable. We must not attempt to put Him in a box or program Him into a computer. "The wind blows where it wishes" (John 3:8). Predicting what God will do is risky. We don't know the future, but we do know the One who holds the future in His hands, and that is all we need to know. Zechariah says, "Not by might nor by power, but by My Spirit, says the Lord of hosts" (Zech. 4:6). God wishes to manifest His power to reach the unreached, and human calculations rob God of His glory. James says, "You do not know what will happen tomorrow" (Jas. 4:14).

The Danger

These arguments are not without weight. They serve a

good purpose in pointing out the dangers of doing the Lord's work in ways not approved by the Lord. It is quite possible for God's servants to become haughty and self-reliant and insensitive to the leading of the Holy Spirit. Numerous examples of this can be cited. Original sin makes us all susceptible to the temptation of taking the glory from God and ascribing it to ourselves. To the extent that such warnings are behind arguments against the desirability of evangelistic soil testing, I want to identify with them.

But the dangers, real as they are, should not cause us to overreact and blind ourselves to spiritually-oriented reasons why intelligent strategy planning for church growth should include some predicting.

Jesus Himself affirmed the ability of the Pharisees and Sadducees to predict the weather by the color of the sky in the morning. Then He called them hypocrites. "You know how to discern the face of the sky, but you cannot discern the signs of the times" (Matt. 16:3). Apparently it is possible for spiritually sensitive persons to discern the signs of the times. The Pharisees and the Sadducees wanted Jesus to give them a spectacular sign from heaven validating His ministry. But Jesus was telling them that they should see God's hand at work in the ordinary development of history around them.

The Reason

One of these ordinary works of God is producing fruit from seed. As I have mentioned before, no human effort can make a seed germinate, grow and produce an eggplant. "God gives the increase" (1 Cor. 3:6). But even in this, God is not irrational or unpredictable.

Take onion farming as an example. Onion farmers

know that if they plant Yellow Globe Hybrids the harvest
will come in 102 days. If they plant White Sweet Spanish it
will take 115 days. If they plant Granex Yellow Hybrid it
will take 170 days. Or take cattle ranchers. They know
that the calf will be born 282 days after the cow is bred.
This is the same gestation period as humans, and usually
God sees to it that it happens.

The Approach

I believe in a balanced approach. What God does is often
predictable, but we also make room for Him to act sover-
eignly and do the unpredictable as well. One of our daugh-
ters was born in six and one-half months instead of nine
months. My wife and I accepted this as something that
God wanted to happen as a variation from the ordinary.
But it was an exception, not the rule.

Making an effort to test the evangelistic soil is not as
new as we may think. It was practiced at least as far back
as A.D. 719 when the great missionary to Europe, Boni-
face, did some soil testing of his own. Look at this fascinating account of yesteryear:

> When the end of April had passed and it was
> already the beginning of May, [Boniface]
> begged and received the apostolic blessing and
> was sent by the Pope to make a report on the
> savage people of Germany. The purpose of this
> was to discover whether their untutored hearts
> and minds were ready to receive the seed of the
> divine Word.[1]

All in all, then, a consensus among professionals in the
field affirms that evangelistic soil testing is desirable. In

fact, George G. Hunter, III, calls it "The Church Growth Movement's greatest contribution to this generation's world evangelization."[2] If only partially as valuable as Hunter claims, it obviously is deserving of high consideration in planning strategies of church growth.

_____ Is Soil Testing Possible? _____

The second question relating to soil testing is whether or not it is possible. In agriculture the technology for testing soils has become highly sophisticated. Farmers know the pH of a given field, the texture, the structure and the porosity of the soil, and how much nitrogen, phosphorus and potassium will be needed for a given crop. Evangelistic soil testing is still somewhat more primitive, but nevertheless very helpful for strategy planning.

I dream of the day when some courageous and energetic computer expert will catch the vision of serving God by working out computer programs for evangelistic soil testing. The technology is currently available, at least enough to make a running start. But, to my knowledge, no one has seriously tackled the problem as yet. Meanwhile we continue to do what we can with the instruments and procedures which are available.

A starting point in conceptualizing the task is a resistance-receptivity axis. This concept was first suggested years ago by Donald McGavran, and a number of practitioners have since experimented with and modified it. Edward R. Dayton has produced its most refined form, his axis being used by the Strategy Working Group of the Lausanne Committee for World Evangelization and is the one I most highly recommend. It looks like this:

HIGHLY RESISTANT
TO THE GOSPEL

HIGHLY RECEPTIVE
TO THE GOSPEL

–5 –4 –3 –2 –1   0 +1 +2 +3 +4 +5

Strongly Opposed	Somewhat Opposed	Indifferent	Somewhat Favorable	Strongly Favorable

RESISTANCE/RECEPTIVITY SCALE[3]

Resistant peoples are also called "left end peoples," because they are plotted toward the left end of the axis. By the same token, the receptive are "right end peoples." The axis can be used for plotting whole people groups or subgroups or clans or families or individuals.

Years of research have shown that, among many others, three major indicators of resistance-receptivity stand out and ought to be considered whenever determining where to plot a given people group on the axis. They are (1) where churches are already growing, (2) where people are changing, and (3) among the masses. We will consider these one at a time.

Where Churches Are Already Growing

It sounds almost too elementary to say that receptivity can be expected where churches are already growing. But it needs to be highlighted because many evangelistic planners develop their strategy on the opposite consideration. They determine, on principle, to evangelize in places where churches have not been growing. For those who have a view to the harvest, such may not be the most efficient approach.

Research, not guesses, is needed in order to make an

accurate calculation for strategy planning. But the research methodology is straightforward:

1. Identify geographical areas where churches are growing.

2. Find out what different people groups occupy that given geographical area.

3. Determine among which of the people groups the churches are growing. In most cases, particularly in urban areas, the church growth will be occurring in only one or a few of the many people groups.

4. Calculate the remaining harvest in the people groups where churches are growing. This can be done easily by subtracting the number of practicing Christians from the total population of the given group.

What you discover can be a good point of departure for planning your strategy. Most people who do this are both surprised and challenged by the large number of unchurched people yet remaining in the group. Because churches are growing among them, they are most likely receptive or right end peoples. If these unchurched are truly a ripened harvest, it is a place where the Lord of the harvest might desire to send laborers.

A relatively unproductive approach is to look at a people group where churches are growing and decide that, because they already have Christian churches, they are adequately cared for. This will be true in some occasions. You may find some groups where the number of churches combined with their strong growth momentum will cause you to conclude, correctly, that they in all probability can gather whatever harvest is there. But this will be the exception.

Some become intimidated because they fear that if they join the evangelistic harvest force, those who are already there will be offended. Unfortunately, this happens sometimes. The ones who got there first have staked a claim and they do their best to protect their turf whether or not they themselves have the potential to complete the harvest. But it is unbiblical to keep laborers out of the harvest field. Donald McGavran calls it "dog-in-the-manger comity," and says that it must be resisted.

Ecclesiastical territorialism is a hindrance to the spread of the gospel. Courage is called for. A new team of workers should enter the field with as kindly an attitude as possible and anxious to establish cordial relationships with those already there. But such cordiality should not be regarded as a precondition for evangelistic action. Vision needs to be focused on the lost, not on the churches already there. Remember the shepherd who leaves the 99 and searches for the one which is lost.

I like the attitude of my friend, Pastor Rick Warren, who has planted a vigorously growing Baptist church in South Orange County, California. He freely offers his time, expertise, research and encouragement to other pastors who plan to start new churches there. "I cannot do otherwise," he says. "It would be like two ants arguing about who's going to eat the elephant!"

The Christian and Missionary Alliance learned some years ago in the Philippines how valuable it is to plan strategy on the basis of discerning where churches are already growing. On the large island of Mindanao missionaries had been working for 60 years. Three major groups were found on the island: the tribal peoples in the Davao province, the traditional Roman Catholics around Zamboanga City, and the Muslims in the Sulu province.

In Sulu the Muslims were being evangelized through radio, schools and literature distribution. Two congregations had been formed among the Samal-speaking Muslims.

In and around Zamboanga City another two congregations had been established during the 60 years, mostly from immigrants arriving from other parts of the Philippines.

In the Davao province, 72 churches had been planted. People from at least one unreached tribe, the Mansakan, sent word to the Christians requesting the gospel of Jesus be brought to their tribe.

Those facts surfaced in a church growth survey done by one of the Alliance missionaries, Joseph Arthur. It was also discovered that, at the time of the survey, all the missionaries had been assigned to Sulu and the Zamboanga area, and none were being sent to Davao province, where, to follow our agricultural analogy, the fruit was so ripe it was falling off the trees.

True to its reputation as one of the more missiologically sensitive mission agencies, the Alliance began to redeploy workers. While they did not neglect the other areas, they concentrated more on the Davao tribal area. The results? In less than 10 years from the time the survey was made they had between 950 and 1000 churches among the tribes. And, as frosting on the cake, they had seven churches in Sulu and 14 churches in Zamboanga, over four times as many in 10 years than they had been able to plant during the first 60.

Where People Are Changing

The first indicator of receptivity is where churches are already growing. The second is where people are changing.

The nature of the change is not as significant as the change itself. It can be social change, political change, economic change, psychological change. These can be produced by war, internal migrations, natural disasters, land reform, change of residence, recessions, revolutions, urbanization, industrialization and many other causes.

The changes might be national, regional, or local. They might affect entire national populations, specific people groups, families or individuals.

For individuals and families, the Holmes-Rahe Stress Scale is a useful tool to identify the kinds of events which may produce change in the individual. It lists 43 life events for adults which cause varying degrees of stress, beginning with death of a spouse valued at 100 points, and then things like divorce, jail term, fired at work, pregnancy, change of work, health—just as examples. Adaptations of the scale have been made for different categories of younger people.[4]

Win Arn says, "A proven principle of church growth is that unchurched people are more responsive to becoming Christians and responsible church members during periods of transition." During these periods they are experiencing certain needs. So, as Arn says, "These and other times of transition in the lives of unchurched individuals are great opportunities for ministering to people in need."[5] Locating people whose needs Jesus can meet is part of sound evangelistic strategy planning.

On a larger scale, Argentina is currently one of the world's flash points of church growth. This was not always true. Throughout most of this century, evangelical church growth in Argentina had lagged far behind most other Latin American countries. Then in 1982 the generals who were in power decided to invade the Falkland Islands, known by them as the Malvinas. Few people outside of Argentina realize what a severe blow the loss of the subsequent war with England was to Argentine national pride.

But it definitely was a socio-psychological turning point for them. The nation underwent a major historical change, and since then the gospel has been spreading and churches have been growing and multiplying at amazing rates across the board.

Central America is another contemporary flash point of church growth, especially Guatamala and Nicaragua. Studies have shown that the accelerated rates of growth in both those countries can be traced back to their respective earthquakes. The earthquakes created instant needs, the evangelicals were sensitive enough and sufficiently able to locate the resources to help meet those needs. The result? Large numbers of people became receptive to the gospel as a result. Again, change has helped to ripen the harvest.

Japanese Christians speak nostalgically of the "seven wonderful years." They refer to the seven years immediately following World War II when the American military was occupying the country. The Japanese had considered their emperor a god, and the war was a holy war for them. Then they lost, and the emperor admitted that he was no god at all. A spiritual vacuum was created which allowed Japanese Christianity to experience its greatest growth in modern times.

During the Vietnam War, the Christian and Missionary Alliance invited church growth consultant Malcolm Bradshaw to do a survey. His report is a model of evangelistic soil testing. He concluded that "Vietnamese war refugees present one of the greatest opportunities in the national church's history for rapid church growth." He recommended that the mission and the national church plan immediate strategies to reach the refugees.[6]

They did. Here is a typical report of exciting evangelistic efforts among the Stieng refugees:

> Bible school students at Dalat spent a week of intensive evangelism among the 11,000 Stieng tribesmen who have been resettled midway between Saigon and Dalat. In that week 1,400 turned to the Lord, raising to 5,000 the number of Stiengs who have become Christians.

Then the report goes on to say the most significant thing for our purposes here: "Until April 1972, when the Viet Cong offensive on the An Loc area pushed them from their ancestral lands, the Stieng tribe was resistant to the gospel."[7] When the people changed, even though it was a forced change, they moved toward the right end of the resistance-receptivity axis. Undoubtedly the change had a great deal to do with traditional tribal spirits who kept them in bondage in the ancestral lands, but whose power was at least partially broken by the move into another geographical area.

Among the Masses

The third indicator of receptivity to the gospel is that, to use Donald McGavran's terminology, the masses are usually more receptive than the classes. The masses refer to the common, working people and the poor. The classes refer to those comfortably situated in power.

Much strategy planning for church growth assumes that if we first attempt to evangelize the higher levels of the social strata in a given area, the gospel will almost automatically trickle down from them to the masses. It has seldom turned out that way. Rather, as historians of the quality of Arnold Toynbee have observed, religion usually enters society among the masses and works its way up.

The phenomenon of the receptivity of the masses needs a bit of qualification, however. Research has shown that worldwide it is valid. But specific exceptions should be recognized. For example, receptivity in the United States seems to cut across class lines. Many upper middle and upper class Americans are ready to receive the gospel. In England it appears that the working class is quite resistant, at least to the way the gospel is currently coming through to them. There may be some other parts of the world where the rule does not apply.

When I served as a missionary in Latin America during the '50s and '60s, the vast majority of evangelicals were counted among the masses. It was a rare thing to find an evangelical church made up of people from the upper classes. Oh, a medical doctor might accept Christ here and a lawyer or school principal there, but not many. Now in the '80s, however, the picture is different. The vigorous church growth continues among the masses. But the classes have also turned receptive, and now hardly a sizeable city in Latin America is without at least one church made up mostly of professionals and fairly well-off people.

Sometimes this lesson has been learned through trial and error as in the case of the Regions Beyond Missionary Union in San Jose de Sisa, Peru. Like many towns in the Andean region, this one contained two kinds of people. The Spanish-speaking mestizos (persons of mixed blood) were the classes. And the Quechua Indians were the masses.

The missionaries operated on the assumption, very common in missionary work in those days, that they should aim for the mestizos who controlled the commerce, the transportation and the government of the town. Once they were won, the Quechuas who were the peasants and the common laborers would follow suit.

In 20 years, this approach had netted six converts.

With this kind of discouraging experience, it might have been reasonable to conclude that San Jose de Sisa belonged over to the left end of the resistance-receptivity axis. It was rocky soil. A green harvest field. But this conclusion would have been wrong. While the mestizos were quite resistant, the Quechuas, as it turned out, were receptive. But the missionaries were not trying to harvest the Quechua field.

Things changed when Victor Cenepo, a Bible school dropout, was sent to San Jose de Sisa because at the time there were no missionaries to send. He was small of stature, slightly crippled and not an eloquent speaker. As to his ministry target, he had no choice. He was a Quechua and the mestizos wouldn't give him the time of day. So he began preaching to the Quechuas in the Quechua language. Four individuals from one family decided for Christ the first night, and soon their entire family was Christian. In eight years, one-third of the village had been converted and was in the church. And as this was happening, several mestizos, more than during the previous 20 years, had given their hearts to Christ.

Although we don't know for sure, it may well have been that the Quechuas would have responded to a ministry such as Victor Cenepo's 10 or 20 years previously. This is not to criticize the missionaries who in those days knew nothing about modern technology for planning strategies of church growth. But it does send a signal to present-day Christian workers in similar situations.

_____ The Harvest Can Pass _____

As farmers well know, the harvest does not last forever. Some crops, such as oranges, can be harvested over a period of time, but others, such as cauliflower, need to be taken at a precise point of ripeness. A wheat field, ready for the harvest, can be wiped out by a hail storm if the combines do not arrive in time.

Evangelistic harvests show similar characteristics. When South Viet Nam fell in the late '70s, a large number of Vietnamese emigrated to the United States. When they first arrived they were quite receptive to the gospel. They were a ripened harvest field. But after a few years, receptivity began to wane, and they began to move from the right end toward the left side of the axis.

I mentioned Japan's "seven wonderful years" in a previous section. For the next 30 years Japan became one of the most difficult of all the mission fields. Materialism and prosperity had filled the vacuum and few were interested in the Christian message. The harvest had passed. There are some encouraging indications that a new time of harvest might be arriving in Japan. Let us hope so and be ready to move in with new workers if it happens.

Donald McGavran tells of a fascinating, but tragic, incident which took place in India over 50 years ago. The London Missionary Society had staffed a mission station in Mirzapur for 100 years. The church had not grown. Converts were few and far between. Then a wave of receptivity touched the Chamars, a people group belonging to the depressed classes. Their leaders came to the missionaries and told them that they wanted to turn from their Hindu idols and follow Jesus Christ.

After long periods of consultation the missionaries made a decision. They said, "These Chamars want to become Christians because they are poor, sick and ignorant. They are heavily in debt. Their children cannot attend the town schools. They have no hope. These are not good reasons to become Christians. Let us first minister to their needs and then let them decide for spiritual reasons to become Christians."

The missionaries began social work among them, and their condition in life improved considerably. But, to their dismay, the missionaries found that the social and material prosperity had moved the Chamars from the right end of the resistance-receptivity axis toward the left. When they finally invited them to become Christians they found that the Chamars had changed their minds and decided to remain Hindu. The harvest had ripened, and then passed. A generation, and probably more than one, had received some hope for this life, but had missed out on hope for the life to come.[8]

Hold the Resistant Lightly

As I mentioned previously, virtually every discussion about the principle of the harvest or resistance and receptivity raises the concern about the resistant. Missionaries have been working among specific people groups for years with little or no harvest. Nor do they anticipate a harvest in the near future. Are these missionaries out of the will of God? Should we abandon people such as Muslims? Do we bypass the unresponsive?

These excellent questions need to be brought out into the open. It is at this very point that some have rejected not only the harvest principle, but the entire Church Growth Movement as well.

No church growth advocate I know has ever suggested that we bypass the resistant. The Great Commission says that we are to preach the gospel to all creatures. Donald McGavran from the beginning has taught that we should "occupy fields of low receptivity lightly."[9] In many cases Christian workers can do nothing more than establish a friendly presence and quietly sow the seed. God continues to call many of his servants to do just that, and I am one who supports and encourages them.

I clearly recall that, soon after I became a Christian over 30 years ago, I was challenged to pray for Christy Wilson in Afghanistan. I didn't know Christy Wilson then (we have become personal friends since), but I prayed for him for years. He and his wife were among the very few missionaries in Afghanistan. Afghans who accepted Christ faced the death penalty. Wilson was able to build a church primarily for non-Afghans, but it was soon bulldozed down by the government. He hung in there for years, and I have always said that we need more Christy Wilsons.

It only makes sense that in countries like Afghanistan we do not need heavy concentrations of missionaries such as we might, for example, in Papua New Guinea. As farmers know, reaping the harvest requires a larger labor force than sowing the seed, and Jesus told us to pray for laborers for the harvest fields. But the seed must be sown and the fields must be watched. If a place like Afghanistan turns ripe, we need someone with the expertise of a Christy Wilson who is on the scene and who can let us know.

_____ What to Do If There Is No Fruit _____

Some Christian workers find that their efforts in evangelism and church growth do not seem to pay off. A great deal of energy is invested with scant returns on the investment. Much seed is sown with little harvest. Frustration is often a positive emotion, particularly when it causes one to pause and take stock of the real situation. If you find yourself in a situation characterized by little or no fruit, I suggest you carefully examine four crucial areas:

1. *Be sure you are in the vine.* I am alluding to Jesus' teaching of the vine and the branches in John 15. This is the spiritual dimension of planning strategies for church growth, and it must not be ignored or avoided. Jesus says, "You did not choose Me, but I chose you and appointed you that you should go and bear fruit, and that your fruit should remain" (John 15:16). He also says, "I am the vine, you are the branches" (John 15:5). In grape production, all grapes grow on branches, none on the vine. So I understand Jesus to be saying that He does not intend to bear fruit directly, but that we, as the branches, are to bear all the fruit.

But the only branches which bear fruit are those locked into the vine. The branches have no power to bear fruit, so they must derive their power from the vine. One cause of fruitlessness, then, could be that we are not locked into Jesus as the branch is locked into the vine. Intimacy with the Saviour is a must. If we are not open channels for the power of the Holy Spirit to flow through us as He wills, we cannot expect to bear much fruit. I realize that all problems in implementing strategies for church growth are not spiritual. But, make no mistake about it, some are. Checking out our relationship to Jesus Christ is a good starting point for troubleshooting a lack of fruit.

2. *Be sure you are preaching to the right people.* Most of this chapter has addressed this matter, so I do not need to elaborate any more. However, to include it in the checklist is necessary.

It is also necessary to recognize that at times God calls workers specifically to certain places or peoples. There may be fruit or there may not. If the call has come clearly—and God uses different ways to communicate His call to different people—the call then comes before the question of fruit. Obedience to God is the highest principle in strategy planning. How frequently this type of direct leading occurs I do not know. Macedonian-type visions are relatively uncommon. It might well be that God desires to do more direct leading than many of us are used to, and if this is the case, the kind of intimacy with God that I spoke about in the previous point becomes even more important.

3. *Be sure you are using the right methods.* One of the dangers in using the resistance-receptivity axis is that you can come to the conclusion that a given people group is resistant to the gospel because they haven't responded when, as a matter of fact, they have been receptive all along, but you have been using the wrong methods for reaching them. It is like a farmer who goes into a beautifully ripe field of wheat with a corn picker. Any farmer who did that would come out empty-handed.

Sometimes the approach to people is faulty. It is important to know how the decision-making process functions in a given society before approaching them with the gospel. I heard of one case in Irian Jaya, for example, when the missionaries made the mistake of sharing the gospel with the children before they shared with the elders of the tribe, and they almost lost their lives.

Sometimes the focus of the message as it is being preached is not relevant to the listeners. In another case in Irian Jaya, Don Richardson found that the Sawi people seemed resistant to his preaching until he told them that Jesus was a "peace child." That was all it took for them to open their hearts to the Holy Spirit. Richardson uses it as an example of the redemptive analogy, and argues that similar God-given points on which to focus the message exist in numerous people groups.

Sometimes communication is at fault. The message is not getting through. Missionaries worked for 25 years with the Tiv tribe in Central Nigeria and saw only 25 baptized believers as a result. Their medium of communication was preaching, which they had learned in Bible school was the way to evangelize. A few years ago some young Tiv Christians set the gospel story to musical chants, the native medium of communication. Almost immediately the gospel began to spread like wildfire, and soon a quarter-million Tiv were worshiping Jesus. The Tiv were not as resistant as the missionaries thought. A change in method brought abundant fruit.

Methods are extremely important around the middle zone of the resistance-receptivity axis. On the left end, virtually no method will reach the highly resistant. On the right end many of them can be won even with poor or careless methods. But, as Donald McGavran says, "In the mid-ranges of the axis, method is of supreme importance. Winnable people may be lost by one method and gained by another."[10]

Because of the crucial need to balance tests for correct methodology over against presumed resistance, it is helpful to distinguish, as does Roy Pointer, between emic resistance and etic resistance,[11] or to use more familiar terms, general resistance and specific resistance. General (or emic) resistance is caused by factors within the group or individual we are trying to reach. In many cases there is little or nothing we can do about such resistance. But specific (or etic) resistance has to do with the individual or group doing the evangelizing. It is here that we can exert some control by changing the evangelizers or by changing the methods. If wise adjustments are made, the resistance may dissolve.

4. *Be sure you are working hard enough.* Most evangelists and missionaries are hard workers, but some are not. And some who work hard do not work smart. They use large amounts of time majoring on the minors. I am

not advocating that we become workaholics. Part of intelligent time management is to build in significant blocks of time for leisure. But I am pointing out that some Christian workers have a lazy streak, and yielding to this can mean a reduction in the fruit that a given ministry produces.

Seeing little or no fruit in your ministry? Measure your present efforts against this four-point checklist and see if it helps your harvest shortfall.

NOTES

1. C.H. Talbot, *The Anglo-Saxon Missionaries in Germany* (New York: Sheed and Ward, 1954), p. 39.
2. George G. Hunter, III, *The Contagious Congregation: Frontiers in Evangelism and Church Growth* (Nashville: Abingdon Press, 1979), p. 104.
3. Edward R. Dayton, *That Everyone May Hear,* 2nd ed. (Monrovia: MARC Publications, 1980), p. 47.
4. Five of these scales are published in *The Win Arn Growth Report,* No. 10, n.d., pp. 2-3.
5. Ibid.
6. Malcolm Bradshaw, "The Vietnamese Church: Is It on the Threshold of Great Expansion?" privately circulated paper, October 1969.
7. *Alliance Witness,* September 19, 1973, p. 12.
8. Donald A. McGavran, *Understanding Church Growth* (Grand Rapids: Wm. B. Eerdmans Publishing Co., 1980), pp. 176-78.
9. Ibid., p. 262.
10. Ibid., p. 261.
11. Roy Pointer, *How Do Churches Grow?* (London: Marshalls, 1984), p. 159.

5
The Meaning of Mission

The way we think about our task makes a great deal of difference in the way we execute it. Edward R. Dayton and David A. Fraser would agree with that statement. In their classic textbook, *Planning Strategies for World Evangelization,* which, incidentally, is an excellent companion volume to this one, they outline a 10-step planning model for going about strategy planning: (1) define the mission, (2) describe the people, (3) describe the force for evangelism, (4) examine means and methods, (5) define an approach, (6) anticipate outcomes, (7) decide our role, (8) make plans, (9) act, (10) evaluate.[1]

Notice that step number one is to define the mission.

I realize that many evangelists and missionaries and other Christian workers are activists. They want to begin with Dayton and Fraser's step number nine. And this is commendable. Without impatient and energetic activists God's work would never get done. But thinking and doing should never be divorced.

Even highly active football players, before taking the field for the game, spend time thinking through a game plan. Far from reducing their action in the game, it makes their action all the more meaningful. The same principle applies to church growth. This is why we need to think through the meaning of mission as an important part of planning church growth strategy.

———— The Kingdom of God and Mission ————

It still seems a little strange to me to begin a discussion of the meaning of mission with the Kingdom of God. Like many evangelicals, I was taught to believe that the Kingdom of God is a future promise which would come some day with the return of the Lord. However, for the better part of 20 years now, a change has been taking place among evangelicals. The theme of the Kingdom of God as a present reality as well as a future promise is becoming much more prominent in evangelical theology than in the past.

Jesus teaches that time can be conceptually divided into "this age" and "the age to come" (Matt. 12:32). The Apostle Paul declares that Jesus is above all principalities and powers "not only in this age but also in that which is to come" (Eph. 1:21). Jesus' second coming separates the two ages. When Jesus returns and ushers in the age to come, the Kingdom of God will have arrived in its fullness. The heavens will pass away, the elements will melt with fervent heat, and the earth will be burned up (see 2 Pet. 3:10). The New Jerusalem will be established, God will reign supreme, and all who are in the New Jerusalem will acknowledge Him as King and obey Him. This is the future reality of the Kingdom.

But we do not need to wait until Christ returns to begin to experience the blessings of the Kingdom of God. The Kingdom invaded this present age when Jesus came the first time. John the Baptist preached in the wilderness of Judea saying, "Repent, for the kingdom of heaven is at hand" (Matt. 3:2). He was preparing the way of the Lord. Then when Jesus began His ministry, His message was "Repent, for the kingdom of heaven is at hand" (Matt. 4:17). When Jesus sent out the Twelve and later the seventy, He told them to preach that the Kingdom of God was at hand. The book of Acts tells of how the apostles preached the Kingdom of God. Several of the Epistles mention the Kingdom of God. Paul reminds the Colossians that God "has delivered us from the power of darkness and translated us into the kingdom of the Son of His love" (Col. 1:13).

Unlike in New Jerusalem, in the present age the "power of darkness," as Paul says, and the Kingdom coexist. And this is where mission comes into the picture. Christian mission is what God sends us to do. He sends us out as ambassadors of His Kingdom into a world yet dominated by the evil one. The resulting conflict between Satan and his forces and God and His forces is the determining characteristic of mission. Victory over Satan is a chief sign of the Kingdom. Jesus says, "If I cast out demons by the Spirit of God, surely the kingdom of God has come upon you" (Matt. 12:28). George Ladd says that this is the "essential theology of the kingdom of God."[2]

On the Damascus Road, the Apostle Paul was called by Jesus to minister to the Gentiles. His future work was described as an invasion into a kingdom dominated by Satan. Paul was "to open their eyes and to turn them from darkness to light, and from the power of Satan to God" (Acts 26:18). Satan is the "god of this age" (2 Cor. 4:4). His power was exhibited in Jesus' temptation. Satan showed Jesus all the kingdoms of the world and said to Him, "All these things I will give You if You will fall down and worship me" (Matt. 4:9). Satan could only do that if they were his to offer. He himself said they were: "This has been delivered to me, and I give it to whomever I wish" (Luke 4:6). The Apostle John later confirms it by saying that "the whole world lies under the sway of the wicked one" (1 John 5:19).

As we have seen in a previous chapter, the heart of the Great Commission is to make disciples of all nations. In the light of the Kingdom of God, each person who becomes a disciple of Jesus Christ is another person lost to the dominion of Satan. That is why the enemy strenuously resists outreach and evangelism and church growth. The Apostle Paul attributes rejection of the gospel directly to the work of the devil: "But even if our gospel is veiled, it is veiled to those who are perishing, whose minds the god of this age has blinded, who do not believe, lest the light of the gospel of the glory of Christ, who is the image of God, should shine on them" (2 Cor. 4:3-4). In the context of the Kingdom of God, mission becomes a venture into spiritual warfare.

———— Mission Demands Holistic Ministry ————

Jesus taught us to pray, "Your kingdom come. Your will be done on earth as it is in heaven" (Matt. 6:10). I understand this as meaning that we, as God's representatives here on earth, are to reflect the values of His kingdom in our lives and ministries. This does not mean that we bring the future Kingdom or the New Jerusalem to earth through our efforts. Only God will do this through supernatural intervention. The New Jerusalem will come only after Satan is cast into the lake of fire and brimstone for good (see Rev. 20:10). Meanwhile we live, as bona fide citizens of the Kingdom of God, in a world yet dominated by the evil one.

What are some of the characteristics of the future Kingdom that should be reflected through us and our churches today? For one thing, no one in the New Jerusalem is lost: "They shall be His people" (Rev. 21:3). Furthermore, "God will wipe away every tear from their eyes; there shall be no more death, nor sorrow, nor crying; and there shall be no more pain" (Rev. 21:4). The evil that we see in the world manifested by sickness and poverty and oppression and exploitation and demonization and immorality and murder is to be vigorously combated in the name of Jesus.

When Jesus sent out His twelve disciples, He told them to do what He had been doing: "Preach, saying, 'The kingdom of heaven is at hand.' Heal the sick, cleanse the lepers, raise the dead, cast out demons" (Matt. 10:7-8). This is what is known as holistic ministry. It aims for the good of the whole person. It seeks not only to save souls, but to help people enjoy a foretaste of the Kingdom in their present lives. Since this is what God sends us to do, this is what mission is all about.

The Two Mandates

As we look at holistic mission more closely, it is helpful to see it made up of what my colleague, Arthur Glasser, calls the two mandates: the cultural mandate and the evangelistic mandate.

The Cultural Mandate

The cultural mandate, which some refer to as Christian social responsibility, goes as far back as the Garden of Eden. After God created Adam and Eve, He said to them: "Be fruitful and multiply; fill the earth and subdue it; have dominion over the fish of the sea, over the birds of the air, and over every living thing that moves on the earth" (Gen. 1:28). As human beings, made in the image of God, we are held accountable for the well-being of God's creation.

In the New Testament we are told that we are to love our neighbors as ourselves (see Matt. 22:39). The concept of neighbor, as the parable of the good Samaritan teaches, includes not only those of our own race or culture or religious group, but all of humanity. Doing good to others, whether our efforts are directed toward individuals or to society as a whole, is a biblical duty, a God-given cultural mandate.

The Evangelistic Mandate

The evangelistic mandate is first glimpsed also in the Garden of Eden. For a period of time, whenever God went to the garden, Adam and Eve were there waiting for Him, and they enjoyed immediate fellowship. But sin entered into the picture. Satan gained his first major victory. The very next time that God went to the garden, Adam and Eve were nowhere to be found. Fellowship had been broken. The human race had been alienated from God. God's nature, in light of the events, was made clear by His next words to Adam—a question: "Where are you?" (Gen. 3:9). He immediately began seeking Adam.

The evangelistic mandate reflects God's desire for fellowship. It involves seeking and finding lost men and women, alienated from God by sin. Romans 10 tells us that whoever calls on the name of the Lord will be saved. But they cannot call if they have not believed and they cannot believe if they have not heard and they cannot hear without a preacher. "How beautiful are the feet of those who preach the gospel of peace" (Rom. 10:15). Bearing the gospel which brings people from darkness to light is implementing the evangelistic mandate. It is what Jesus intended when He sent out His followers to "make disciples of all nations" (Matt. 28:19). It is the Great Commission.

One Mission—Two Parts

Both Christian social ministry and evangelism are essential parts of biblical mission. We use the term "mandates" to indicate that both are mandatory, never optional. There is a growing consensus on this point in evangelical circles.

This consensus, however, is comparatively recent. Prior to the 1960s most evangelicals equated mission with the evangelistic mandate. This is not to say that they ignored social or material needs. Evangelicals have always been involved in meeting human need. But while this activity may have been a means toward evangelization or a fruit of salvation, it was not considered part of mission itself.

I could cite many examples of this perception, but none perhaps as prominent as the Berlin World Congress on Evangelism sponsored by the Billy Graham Evangelistic Association and *Christianity Today* in 1966. With the exception of a minor address by Paul Rees of World Vision, there was virtually no mention in Berlin of the cultural mandate. In Berlin, John R. W. Stott, widely recognized as a principal evangelical spokesperson, said, "The commission of the church is not to reform society, but to preach the Gospel."[3] In his analysis of the trends, Arthur Johnston says that Berlin "stood firm on proclamation evangelism as *the* mission of the church."[4]

One of the first evangelicals to stress the cultural mandate in a public forum was Horace Fenton of the Latin

America Mission at the Wheaton Congress on the Church's Worldwide Mission, also held in 1966. In his address, "Mission—and Social Concern," he argued that it was unbiblical to separate the two mandates (although he did not use that terminology) in defining the mission of the church.[5]

Fenton was one of the pioneers, but the rest of the evangelical world had begun to catch up by 1974 when the International Congress on World Evangelization was held at Lausanne, Switzerland. At Lausanne the cultural mandate was given a relatively high profile in the plenary sessions. By then John Stott himself had changed his views, recognizing that mission contained both the cultural and the evangelistic mandates. The resulting *Lausanne Covenant* (see Appendix) makes a strong statement on the cultural mandate in Article 5, and on the evangelistic mandate in Articles 4 and 6.

_____ **Where Is the Priority?** _____

The next question is that of priority, and this is a crucial point for planning strategies of church growth.

There are five major positions on priority in today's debate: (1) Some would say that mission involves the cultural mandate only. We are not about the business of proselyting people to our faith. (2) Others prioritize the cultural mandate over the evangelistic mandate. (3) Others give equal weight to both mandates and refuse to prioritize either. (4) Others prioritize the evangelistic mandate over the cultural mandate. (5) The final group holds the pre-Lausanne view that mission is the evangelistic mandate, period.

Most evangelicals find themselves at positions three, four or five. In my opinion, position four is the most helpful for planning strategies for church growth. I believe we must minister to the whole person: body, soul and spirit. Both mandates must be obeyed, but the evangelistic mandate is primary. I hold this position not only for pragmatic reasons, but also because I find it thoroughly biblical.

Again, the biblical reasons go back to the Garden of Eden. God told Adam and Eve that they could eat from all the trees except one. If they ate from the tree of the knowledge of good and evil they would die (see Gen. 2:17). Satan tempted them, they ate the forbidden fruit, and they died. But Adam and Eve did not drop over on the spot like Ananias and Sapphira. So, in what sense did they die? They died in three senses: spiritually, physically and materially or socially. Let's examine them in reverse order.

1. *Material or social death.* In the Garden of Eden all of Adam and Eve's material needs were met with little or no effort. But Satan succeeded in tempting them and sin put an end to that. They were driven from the garden, and God cursed the ground. Thorns and thistles began to grow, and from then on they would get food only through the sweat of their brow and have babies only with considerable pain. This was the beginning of the myriad of social and material problems that humans have experienced through the years: poverty, war, oppression, discrimination, slavery, social injustice, famine.

And how long will these problems last? They will be with us until Jesus returns and establishes the New Jerusalem. God sent cherubim to keep Adam and Eve from access to the Garden of Eden and the tree of life. But the tree of life will be there once again in the New Jerusalem (see Rev. 22:2). Meanwhile, as Jesus said, the poor will be with us always. Material or social death is a constant reminder of Satan's presence and activity. So what do we,

as Christians, do about it? We fulfill the cultural mandate.
We love our neighbor as ourselves. We follow Jesus'
example when He said, "The Spirit of the Lord is upon
Me, because He has anointed Me to preach the gospel to
the poor" (Luke 4:18).

2. *Physical death*. Before the Fall, Adam and Eve
were immortal. Sickness and death were not a part of the
Garden of Eden. But, while Adam and Eve did not die
instantly when they sinned, the immediate result was that
they became mortal. Physical death became inevitable,
and, of course, they both eventually expired—a direct
result of the efforts of Satan.

In the New Jerusalem, as we mentioned earlier, there
is no more death nor sorrow nor pain (see Rev. 21:4). But
meanwhile we live in a world where sickness and pain and
physical death are constant reminders of Satan's presence
and influence. What do we, as Christians, do about it?
Again, we fulfill the cultural mandate. We do the best we
can to alleviate these areas of human suffering. We train
surgeons, we encourage medical research, we produce
therapeutic drugs, we build hospitals. We also draw on
supernatural resources which God has promised us. Jesus'
agenda included not only preaching the gospel to the poor,
but "recovery of sight to the blind" (Luke 4:18). We lay
hands on the sick, pray for them, and expect to see some
healed.

3. *Spiritual death*. Spiritual death is the most serious
of all three. It is the separation of human beings from God.
I have already described the scenario in the Garden of
Eden where fellowship between God and humans was broken, much to the delight of Satan. Why do I say it is the
most serious of all?

Notice that material and social problems are temporal,
and so are their solutions. We can feed the starving in

Africa, we can emancipate the slaves, we can institute legislation for land reform, we can sign international peace treaties, and we should do all of those things. This is part of our Christian duty. But none of those solutions is permanent. The problems will keep recurring until we get to the New Jerusalem.

The same thing applies to ministry in the supernatural. We can heal the sick, we can perform signs and wonders in Jesus' name, we can cast out demons. But none of those things is permanent. Everyone whom Jesus healed eventually died. Even Lazarus, whom Jesus raised from the dead, later died.

In contrast to these temporary measures, the solution for spiritual death is not temporal, but eternal. When a lost person is born again and follows Jesus Christ and reestablishes fellowship with the Father, it lasts forever. Whoever believes in Jesus will not perish, but have everlasting life (see John 3:16). Helping to bring this about is fulfilling the evangelistic mandate. It is primarily what Jesus came and died for. "The Son of Man has come to seek and to save that which was lost" (Luke 19:10).

The Evangelical Debate

It is for these reasons, which I think are quite substantial, that I adhere to position four: mission includes both the cultural and the evangelistic mandates, but we should prioritize the evangelistic mandate. I have great respect for my evangelical colleagues who argue for position three, namely that both mandates should be given equal weight. Some, such as my good friend Harvie Conn, object even to thinking abstractly about two mandates. He says, "It is not an either/or, not a both/and, not even a simply primary/secondary." Later, Conn explains, "They are not basically two mandates but two stages in God's covenant relationship with man."[6]

I have no intention of entering into polemics and attempting to prove that those who disagree are wrong. The concerns they are representing have much value, and I want to identify with their compassion for the poor and oppressed. Nevertheless, I do not believe social concern is the best starting point either theologically or pragmatically for planning strategies for church growth. It is better to include both, but to prioritize evangelism.

Over the period of a decade this issue has been debated in three international evangelical consultations, and each one has affirmed the priority of evangelism. The first was the International Congress on World Evangelization at Lausanne in 1974. The *Lausanne Covenant* (see Appendix) affirms both mandates, as I have mentioned previously, but says in Paragraph 6: "In the church's mission of sacrificial service, evangelism is primary." The second was the Consultation on World Evangelization held in Pattaya, Thailand in 1980. The emphasis of Lausanne, prioritizing evangelism, was specifically reaffirmed.

The third consultation was called because vocal minorities at both Lausanne and Pattaya strongly objected to prioritizing the evangelistic mandate. The Theology Working Group of the Lausanne Committee joined the Theological Commission of the World Evangelical Fellowship in convening the Consultation on the Relationship between Evangelism and Social Responsibility in Grand Rapids, Michigan in 1982 in order to bring together representatives of the evangelical spectrum. Once again, the priority of evangelism was affirmed, but not before a strong recognition that the cultural mandate is an indispensable component of Christian mission.

Two important forms of Christian social responsibility

are highlighted in the 64-page *Grand Rapids Report*. Social *service* entails meeting immediate needs in relief and development activities. Social *action* means taking steps to improve oppressive and unjust social structures. Following that, in one of the first such statements in a broadly evangelical document, mention is made of the role of supernatural power in healing the sick and casting out demons as a part of implementing the cultural mandate.

Social ministry relates to evangelism in three principal ways, according to the report. Social activity is a *consequence* of evangelism. People experiencing new life in Christ reach out in love to their neighbors. Faith is demonstrated by works (see James 2:18). Social activity is also a *bridge* to evangelism. A tangible expression of Christian love to unbelievers can open hearts to the gospel. And finally, social activity is a *partner* of evangelism. While they are distinct from one another, every evangelistic act has social implications and every act of Christian mercy has evangelistic implications.

Then the report goes on to point out that, while any number of human agencies can engage in social activities, when it comes to bringing the good news of salvation, "Christians are doing what nobody else can do." Our hope is that we would never have to make the choice between satisfying physical hunger and spiritual hunger. "Nevertheless, if we must choose, then we have to say that the supreme and ultimate need of all humankind is the saving grace of Jesus Christ, and that therefore a person's eternal, spiritual salvation is of greater importance than his or her temporal and material well-being."[7]

———— **What Does the Priority Mean?** ————

The basic reason for this lengthy discussion of the meaning of mission is to underscore its importance in planning strategies for church growth. While there have been numerous cases of Christian social ministries and evangelism enjoying a symbiotic relationship, each helping the other, there are also some cases where it has not worked out well and where social activity has actually hindered church growth. I will grant that there may be unusual circumstances in which, due to disastrous social conditions, the best Christian decision might be to reverse the priorities temporarily. But I am regarding this as an exception, not the rule. The rule is that we attempt to avoid involvement in social activities which predictably can reduce our evangelistic effectiveness. We cannot afford to sell our birthright for a pot of stew.

The most dramatic membership decline in the history of the mainline Protestant denominations in America began in the mid-1960s and has continued for 20 years. During the first 10 years of the decline the denominations in question paid little attention to what was happening. But more recently they have become concerned and are studying the causes.

Having been part of a high-level consortium that dealt with this concern from 1976 to 1978, I have given a good deal of thought to the problem of membership decline. I wish to avoid oversimplifying causes of church growth and decline, for I am fully aware of the interplay of contextual and institutional factors; of local and regional and national factors; of spiritual and sociological factors. But my conclusion is—and many others would agree—that the primary cause of the decline in mainline membership was a subtle priority shift.

Prior to the '60s the evangelistic mandate was high on the agendas of the major denominations. The '50s was a decade of vigorous church growth. But due to the effects of the social upheavals of the '60s such as the Viet Nam War, the civil rights movement and the rise of the hippie counterculture, the influential members of the denominational bureaucracies began to prioritize the cultural mandate. The United Presbyterians, for example, decided to allocate $10,000 of their mission funds to Angela Davis's defense. Mission came to mean jumping on the bandwagon of the newest liberal political cause to the neglect of evangelism and church planting. The results, in terms of church growth, were strongly negative.

The mainline denomination which has lost most members is the United Methodists, showing a decrease of some 2 million in 20 years. Now some Methodist leaders, such as Bishop Richard B. Wilkie, are speaking out strongly concerning priorities. Wilkie quotes John Wesley as saying, "We have nothing to do but save souls." This, he rightly points out, is not to deny the social witness, but is simply helping to put matters in the right perspective.

"We have become preoccupied with politics," Wilkie laments. "We have forgotten how to mediate the change which God works in the heart through faith in Christ."[8] Partially as a result of this, Wilkie points out that "the public pronouncements of our boards and agencies—even those of the Council of Bishops—now have little power." The reason? "First of all we are now a smaller denomination with less influence."[9]

During those same 20 years when mainline denominations were shifting their mission focus, many other American denominations, mostly newer ones, held firm to their existing priorities. Those groups, such as Southern Baptists, Church of God (Cleveland), Church of the Nazarene, Assemblies of God, independent charismatic churches and others, maintained strong growth while the rest lost members. The growing groups had continued to prioritize evangelism. They had understood the meaning of mission.

Previously, I recounted Donald McGavran's story of the Chamars in Mirazpur, India. The Chamars, as a group, expressed to the missionaries a desire to leave their Hindu gods and follow Jesus Christ. Then the missionaries made a basic mistake. They prioritized the cultural mandate and decided they should help the Chamars improve their social and material lot first. Afterwards, they could evangelize them and allow them to enter the Kingdom. The results, we noted, were disastrous. By the time they were socially and materially comfortable, the Chamars had lost interest in following Jesus and were more attached than ever to their Hindu gods.

Evangelism Is the Magnet

I like to think of the evangelistic mandate as a magnet. When placed above the cultural mandate, it tends to pull them both up. When placed below the cultural mandate, it tends to pull them both down. The National Council of Churches, for instance, had a great deal of social influence in the '50s and '60s. Now their social influence is minimal. Why? They decided to put the evangelistic mandate under the cultural mandate. During the same period of time the National Association of Evangelicals and the National Religious Broadcasters have been gaining social influence in the nation. They kept the evangelistic mandate on the top.

The Gallup Organization became interested in this phenomenon, so they did a national survey asking, "Do you, yourself, happen to be involved in any charity or social service activities such as helping the poor, the sick or the elderly?" Nonevangelical Christians answered positively 26 percent of the time, while evangelical Christians gave a 42 percent positive answer.[10] This was followed up with another Gallup poll with *Christianity Today* yielding similar results. Evangelicals showed up to be considerably higher than other groups in their concern for and involvement in the cultural mandate. [11]

No American mission agency that I am aware of is more zealous for the evangelistic mandate than SIM International, formerly the Sudan Interior Mission. Yet, like almost all other evangelical bodies, they end up furthering the cultural mandate in a significant way. One recent issue of their magazine, *SIM Now*, tells how missionaries helped the people in Niger stop the encroachment of the Sahara Desert through reforestation, established nurseries for tree seedlings, reintroduced the cassava plant for food, cleaned up the water pollution, introduced "low tec" mud stoves, taught poultry management, vaccinated 3,750 chickens and greatly improved the life of the people. Another young missionary woman in Nigeria vaccinated 200,000 cattle belonging to Fulani Muslims against rinderpest. She vaccinated 300 an hour up to 10 hours per day. Now, she says, "It's a rare day when I don't have opportunity to tell them about God's gift of eternal life. I'm their friend now, so they listen."[12]

In planning church growth strategies, plan for both the cultural mandate and the evangelistic mandate. But don't forget that the best way to maximize both is to conceptualize evangelism as the magnet and keep it on top.

NOTES

1. Edward R. Dayton and David A. Fraser, *Planning Strategies for World Evangelization* (Grand Rapids: Wm. B. Eerdmans Publishing Co., 1980), p. 43.
2. George Eldon Ladd, *A Theology of the New Testament* (Grand Rapids: Wm. B. Eerdmans Publishing Co., 1974), p. 66.

3. John R.W. Stott, "The Great Commission" in *One Race, One Gospel, One Task*, ed. Carl F.H. Henry and W. Stanley Mooneyham (Minneapolis: World Wide Publications, 1967), vol. 1, p. 50.
4. Arthur Johnston, *The Battle for World Evangelization* (Wheaton: Tyndale House Publishers, 1978), p. 221.
5. Horace L. Fenton, Jr., "Mission—and Social Concern" in *The Church's Worldwide Mission*, ed. Harold Lindsell (Waco: Word Books, 1966), pp. 193-203.
6. Harvie M. Conn, *Evangelism: Doing Justice and Preaching Grace* (Grand Rapids: Zondervan Publishing House, 1982), p. 63.
7. *Evangelism and Social Responsibility: An Evangelical Commitment*, Grand Rapids Report, Lausanne Occasional Paper No. 21 (Box 1100, Wheaton, IL 60187), p. 25.
8. Richard B. Wilkie, *And Are We Yet Alive?* (Nashville, TN: Abingdon Press, 1986), p. 40.
9. Ibid., p. 37.
10. *Emerging Trends*, Princeton Religious Research Center, January 1979, pp. 1-2.
11. Kenneth L. Wilson, "Concern for Society," *Christianity Today*, October 12, 1980, p. 41.
12. *SIM Now*, March-April 1985, pp. 2-4, 9.

6
The Meaning of Evangelism

If we agree with the *Lausanne Covenant* that "in the church's mission of sacrificial service, evangelism is primary," then it becomes extremely important to know precisely what evangelism is. Many Christians assume that the word "evangelism" is self-explanatory and needs no further elaboration. Even some authors of books on evangelism fall into this trap. I have never done a scientific survey, but I would estimate that in over half the books on evangelism the authors never stop to explain exactly how they are using the word. Like many others, they *assume* a definition of evangelism, and when they do that, they usually assume what I consider an inadequate definition.

In strategy planning in general, as we have seen, setting the goal is a prerequisite to deciding methodologies. Our task is to plan strategies for church growth. Evangelism is an integral part of this. It is necessary, therefore, that we have a clear understanding of just how evangelism and church growth relate. It is also necessary to show how some contemporary definitions of evangelism can hinder, rather than help, the growth of churches.

Are Evangelism and
_____ Church Growth the Same? _____

While evangelism and church growth are closely related, they should not be confused with each other. In American academia there are professional societies for each: the Academy of Evangelism in Theological Education and the North American Society for Church Growth. In my own institution, Fuller Seminary, we have professors of evangelism and professors of church growth, with a series of course offerings in each field.

Church growth means all that is involved in bringing men and women who do not have a personal relationship to Jesus Christ into fellowship with Him and into responsible church membership.[1] That is one of the standard operational definitions of church growth which has become quite popular. But it is not detailed enough to bring out some of the ways that church growth differs from evangelism. The most widely accepted formal definition of church growth is the one which is written into the constitution of the North American Society for Church Growth:

> Church growth is that discipline which investigates the nature, expansion, planting, multiplication, function, and health of Christian churches as they relate to the effective implementation of God's commission to "make disciples of all peoples" (Mt. 28:18-20). Students of church growth strive to integrate the eternal theological principles of God's word concerning the expansion of the church with the best insights of contemporary social and behavioral sciences, employing as the initial frame of reference the foundational work done by Donald McGavran.

It can be seen by that definition that many concerns of church growth are not related to evangelism per se. Church planting is usually not a subset of evangelism. Neither is the process of diagnosing the health of a church. Many aspects of Christian nurture and the assimilation of new members are dealt with in church growth. The fields of spiritual gifts and small group dynamics are important to church growth.

There are three ways in which new members come into a church. *Biological growth* comes from the children of Christian families growing up and going through the specific system devised by the church for bringing young people to Christ and into church membership. Most church growth worldwide comes through biological growth. *Transfer growth* takes place when believers withdraw their membership from one church and affiliate with another church. *Conversion growth* comes from sharing the gospel with unchurched people, bringing them to Christ and into the church.

Evangelism is primarily related to conversion growth. Secondarily, it touches biological growth because in a real sense the children of believers need to be evangelized. But transfer growth is not a concern of evangelism per se. All three, including transfer growth, are important to church growth. For example, if people are transferring out of a given church in large numbers, church growth deals with the problem. Church growth also analyzes why some churches experience healthy transfer growth year after year. In this sense, church growth is broader than evangelism.

But there are also areas of interest to evangelism that do not relate to church growth. As we will see shortly, there are some very popular definitions of evangelism which have little or nothing to do with church growth.

Many professional evangelists are interested in leading souls to Christ, but they are only marginally concerned whether or not the converts get into churches. The field of evangelism also deals in much more detail with specific evangelistic methodologies than does church growth. In these respects, evangelism is broader than church growth.

Popular typologies of evangelism and church growth show where some important overlap takes place. Evangelism can be classified as:

E-0 or evangelism zero is the process of leading people to a commitment to Jesus Christ who are already church members. As this happens, the church does not grow in membership, but it grows in quality.

E-1 or evangelism one means leading people to Christ who are members of the same cultural group. In order to do this you do not have to learn a new language or eat new food or adopt new customs.

E-2 or evangelism two and E-3 or evangelism three both indicate a cross-cultural evangelism. In order to do it, you have to minister in a culture other than your own. E-2 is evangelizing people in a culture similar to your own, like an American evangelizing Germans. E-3 involves a more distant culture such as an American evangelizing Chinese.

Church growth can be classified as:

Internal growth. This refers to an improvement in the quality of a church. Christians grow in their worship, study of the Word of God, caring for each other, fruit of the Spirit, prayer lives and in many other ways. E-0 is included as a part of internal growth, because when unconverted church members are born again, the quality of the church improves.

Expansion growth. This includes reaching out and

bringing new people from the outside into the fellowship of the church whether through conversion or transfer. Since the new people are from the same culture, E-1 fits under expansion growth.

Extension growth. This is a synonym for church planting. The new converts are gathered into new congregations. E-1 also fits here, since no cultural lines are crossed.

Bridging growth. Bridging growth also means planting new churches, but in this case the churches are in different cultures. Both E-2 and E-3 fit into this category, depending on how distant the second culture is from that of those who do the evangelizing.

Because of this overlap, planning strategies for church growth must take evangelism very seriously.

Three Views of Evangelism

The meaning of evangelism, like the meaning of mission, is a point of vigorous debate in today's Christian world.

There are some superficial uses of the term to describe just about anything that is done in and around churches. The word has been used to describe such disparate activities as radio broadcasting, building roads, organizing Sunday School, lobbying in Washington, leading a choir, translating the Bible, coaching basketball, holding mass crusades, feeding hungry people, or explaining the Four Spiritual Laws. Particularly in evangelical circles, anything to which the designation "evangelism" can be attached has a good chance of gaining support, so it is frequently watered down to mean very little. Ironically, in some churches, largely those affiliated with the older mainline denominations, evangelism is considered almost a dirty word. Any activity it is attached to will be in danger of losing support.

But, moving past the superficial use or nonuse of the term, there are three prominent ways that evangelism is described by leaders today. I call them *presence, proclamation* and *persuasion*. The decision you take as to which definition you use as a goal for church growth strategy will usually make a significant difference in the outcome.

Presence Evangelism

Presence evangelism holds that our primary relationship to those outside the faith should be to do good works and help them with any needs that they might have. Giving a cup of cold water is the objective. Sometimes it is given in the name of Jesus Christ, but sometimes not. "Anonymous witness" is acceptable to some advocates of this position.

Many who hold the presence viewpoint argue that our task is not to convert or proselytize non-Christians, but to learn from them and thereby enrich our own faith. We are to help Muslims become better Muslims, but not "force" them to follow Jesus. One author argues that evangelism means doing what is necessary to overcome racism, sexism, classism, ageism and economic imperialism. Another says that if we engage in social action we are thereby doing evangelism. The question of how many of those we minister to actually become disciples of Jesus Christ is not an important issue.

The idea of Christian presence as evangelism can be traced back for 100 years. But the term itself gained considerable popularity in the sixties, particularly among groups affiliated with the World Council of Churches, where, as R. K. Orchard says, it is considered by many as "the basic form of witness."[2]

The idea still holds sway with a considerable number of Christian leaders. A few years ago the National Council of Churches in the United States conducted a survey of ministers from the Reformed Church of America, the United Presbyterian Church (before the merger), the United Methodist Church and the United Church of Christ. Fewer than 40 percent of these clergy believed that the basic purpose of missions was to bring individuals to accept Christ or to save those who do not know Christ. Almost half of the ministers felt that faiths other than Christianity were valid religious options. While they were not asked specifically if they held to "presence evangelism," their responses to the other questions would suggest that this is their approach.

To flash back to the discussion of the meaning of mission, many of those who subscribe to presence evangelism would fall at positions one or two. In other words, they think that mission is entirely the cultural mandate or they prioritize the cultural mandate over the evangelistic mandate. Colin Williams, for example, argues that "the distinction between individual evangelism and evangelism calling for [social] changes is a false one."[3] Needless to say, this is not an evangelical point of view. Few, if any, evangelicals would be satisfied with defining evangelism as Christian presence.

Proclamation Evangelism

Proclamation evangelism goes beyond presence. It agrees that in order to evangelize effectively, a Christian presence must be established. Evangelists must love the people they are ministering to, this love must be demonstrated in both word and deed, and they have to earn the right to be heard. There is no disagreement on the need to do good works. Good works authenticate the gospel. They may even produce evangelistic results as by-products when people "see your good works and glorify your Father in heaven" (Matt. 5:16).

But with all this, doing good works *in itself* should not be called evangelism. Proclamation evangelism says that there is more to it. An essential ingredient in evangelism is verbalizing the message of the gospel of Jesus Christ. It is making the good news of Jesus known in such a way that people will hear and understand it.

It is easy to caricature proclamation evangelism. Joseph Bayly wrote an enjoyable satire years ago entitled *The Gospel Blimp,* and it was later made into a motion picture. He effectively and tastefully caricatured proclamation evangelism, bringing to our attention that evangelism involves more than simply announcing the plan of salvation from a blimp. I once heard the story of Methodist layperson Jewel Pierce of Piedmont, Alabama, who spread the gospel by stuffing whiskey bottles with tracts and floating them down the river. It was a different approach, but he obtained some results. In response to his sending 30,000 bottles downriver, he received back 5,000 letters and has documented one church that started when some people were converted through reading a bottle's contents.

We may chuckle over blimp and whiskey bottle evangelism, but I'm sure also that a part of most of us says with the Apostle Paul, "Christ is preached; and in this I rejoice, yes, and will rejoice" (Phil. 1:18). I bring up blimp and whiskey bottle evangelism simply to say that the kind of proclamation evangelism I am describing in this section is something more substantial than that.

At its best, proclamation evangelism contends that

evangelizing is making known the message of salvation through Jesus Christ in such a way that the unbelievers who hear it will clearly understand it. Once this is done and the unbelievers have heard and understood the gospel, they are considered evangelized. Some will believe the gospel and some will reject it, but whatever their decision, they have been evangelized. A frequent motto of those who hold the proclamation definition of evangelism is "share Christ and leave the results to God."

This view of evangelism is very strong among evangelical Christians. I previously mentioned that many authors of books on evangelism simply assume a definition of evangelism. When they do, nine times out of 10 their definition is proclamation. They feel that it is so commonly accepted it needs no argument.

Most evangelists and evangelistic associations that I am aware of also assume proclamation as their working definition of evangelism. Some of them do not verbalize the definition, but it is implicitly clear from the way they report the results of their evangelistic efforts. The typical report of a single evangelistic crusade or the annual report of an association will feature three figures: (1) the financial report of how much was collected and how it was spent, (2) the number of individuals who attended the meetings, and (3) the number of persons who, in one way or another, indicated their desire to receive Jesus Christ as Lord and Saviour. In the latter figures they are usually quite careful now days to refer to them as "inquirers" rather than "converts." This kind of reporting clearly reflects a proclamation evangelism approach.

Notice how you decide whether a given individual is evangelized under this definition. Suppose, for example, that 50,000 attend a crusade and that 3,000 come forward and pray to receive Christ. How many of those people are

considered evangelized? Some might say that all the unbelievers among the 50,000 were thereby evangelized
because they heard a clear gospel message. Others, if
pressed, might say that only the 3,000 who made decisions were evangelized. Either way, this is what I mean by
proclamation evangelism.

Persuasion Evangelism

Persuasion evangelism goes beyond presence and proclamation. It agrees with proclamation that evangelism does
not take place until the gospel message is meaningfully
made known to unbelievers, but it does not agree that a
person is to be considered evangelized when they simply
hear and understand the gospel message. Persuasion
evangelism says that a person is not regarded as evangelized unless and until he or she becomes a disciple of Jesus
Christ and a responsible member of a local church.

This is the definition which best fits the understanding
of the Great Commission explained in chapter 2. To reiterate, the one imperative out of the four action verbs in Matthew 28:19-20 is "make disciples." "Go," "baptizing" and
"teaching" are all participles in the original Greek. So far
as measuring evangelistic results is concerned, the bottom line is how many disciples are made as the result of a
given evangelistic effort, not how many people hear. And,
as I also brought out in chapter 2, an acceptable criterion
for knowing when a person who makes a decision is really
turning out to be a disciple is that they become a responsible member of the Body of Christ in a local church.

_____ 3-P Evangelism _____

I like to think of the three kinds of evangelism I have just described as three stories of one building. Conceptualizing it in that way helps us see first how the three are related to each other, and secondly what the ultimate goal of evangelism really is.

Presence is the bottom story of the building. It contains the door, the entrance. It is the foundation of the whole process. Through Christian presence a relationship of trust and openness with those who hear the gospel is established. It is absolutely necessary for meaningful evangelism. But some consider presence as evangelism itself. The final goal of evangelism is measured in how many people are helped. This is *1-P evangelism,* and I regard it as an inadequate definition of evangelism.

Proclamation is the second story. I see it as containing the window which lets the light into the building. Verbalizing the gospel message allows the light of salvation in Jesus Christ to shine on those who do not know Christ. This also is essential for effective evangelism. But, again, some consider proclamation as evangelism itself. The final goal of evangelism is measured in how many people hear and understand. This is *2-P evangelism* and I regard it, as well, as an inadequate definition of evangelism.

Persuasion completes the building as the third and final story. It adds the roof. It is not satisfied to think of evangelism as any less than making disciples. It accepts both presence and proclamation as essential parts of the evangelistic process, but not as ends. The final goal of evangelism is measured in how many people validate their decision for Christ by continuing steadfastly in the apostles' doctrine and fellowship and in breaking of bread and prayers. This is *3-P evangelism* and, in my opinion, the most adequate definition for planning strategies of church growth. It is the one definition of the three which relates evangelism directly to church growth.

_____ **The Engel Scale** _____

James Engel of Wheaton College has developed a remarkable instrument for helping to measure progress in the evangelistic process. It is a linear scale which, admittedly, does not appear useful to many from other cultures, particularly some in the two-thirds world. But I am among those who find it very useful in attempting to conceptualize particularly the essential differences between proclamation and persuasion, between 2-P and 3-P evangelism.

The Engel Scale shows eight steps toward an unbeliever becoming a disciple of Jesus Christ and three steps afterward:

-8 Awareness of a supreme being, but no effective knowledge of the gospel
-7 Initial awareness of the gospel
-6 Awareness of the fundamentals of the gospel
-5 Grasp of the implications of the gospel
-4 Positive attitude toward the gospel
-3 Personal problem recognition
-2 Decision to act
-1 Repentance and faith in Christ

The person is regenerated and becomes a new creature.

+1 Post-decision evaluation
+2 Incorporation into the body
+3 A lifetime of conceptual and behavioral growth in Christ

Depending on one's theological orientation, the "repentance and faith in Christ" might be located elsewhere on the scale, but I am dealing here more with strategy than theology. Notice that 2-P evangelism stops at -2, "decision to act." As Engel points out, the decision can either be for acceptance or rejection. If it is rejection, the person moves back to -5 on the scale. But whether it is acceptance or rejection, the person at -2 is considered evangelized according to proclamation evangelism.

Persuasion or 3-P evangelism does not consider the person evangelized until he or she reaches +2 on the Engel Scale, "incorporation into the body." It is only at that point when evangelism ceases and Christian nurture takes over.

For those who hold 2-P evangelism, the area between -2 and +2 is not called evangelism, but "follow-up." Evangelism and follow-up are discreet stages of ministry. Proclamation-oriented evangelists frequently assert their concern that all those who make decisions for Christ in their crusades eventually join local churches. But they do not consider it their *evangelistic* responsibility to see that it happens. They do not measure the success or failure of their crusades on that criterion. They expect others, such as local pastors, to do the follow-up, after they have finished the evangelism. If the inquirers never do find their way into local churches, it is not considered the fault of the evangelist because he or she never assumed that responsibility as a part of the evangelistic ministry.

Research which I have done on evangelism has led me to the conclusion that separating evangelism and follow-up conceptually in the evangelistic design builds a failure factor into the process. This is why I advocate 3-P evangelism. Confirming the new convert's positive decision for Christ and seeing that the person becomes a responsible member of a local church is all part of *evangelism*, not a step to be taken after evangelism is over. If Great Com-

mission or disciple-making evangelism is desired, building
the strategy around persuasion evangelism has great practical advantages.

I have mentioned "responsible membership in a local
church" frequently. A word is needed as to how I am using
the word "church." In this context I am giving it a broad
meaning. I am referring to a group of believers in Christ
who are committed to each other and who meet regularly
to worship and minister and study the Word of God and
pray and grow in their Christian lives. Ordinarily it takes
the form of a local church, but it could be a Campus Crusade group at a university or a home Bible study group or
an adult Sunday School class or any other such group.

One practical recent illustration of what happens when
a 2-P definition of evangelism is used is seen in the prestigious *World Christian Encyclopedia,* edited by my friend
David Barrett. Barrett and I have been in personal dialogue over the definition of evangelism for many years. He
has persistently maintained the proclamation point of view.
In the *Encyclopedia* Barrett says, "The word evangelization is often used incorrectly, as if it were synonymous
with conversion or christianization." What Barrett refers
to as incorrect is roughly my point of view and that of persuasion evangelism.

He goes on to say that the *Encyclopedia* uses the term
"in a broader sense to mean the spreading of the Good
News."[4] So what does this imply in concrete terms? It
means that, to use some examples from the *Encyclopedia,*
Saudi Arabia is 32 percent evangelized, Egypt is 58 percent evangelized, Bangladesh is 60 percent evangelized,
Russia is 71 percent evangelized, Taiwan is 89 percent
evangelized and the United States, Brazil, France, South
Africa and Zaire are 100 percent evangelized. Some will
say that they disagree that the United States is 100 per-

cent evangelized. So do I. But they must realize that Barrett's conclusion is consistent with his 2-P definition of evangelism.

———— Is "Persuasion" the Best Word? ————

I don't like the word "persuasion" very much. For one thing, to attach it to 3-P evangelism is all right, but it must be understood that many who hold to proclamation evangelism would also agree that persuasion should be used in evangelizing. They believe in strong, persuasive proclamation. So it could be somewhat confusing at that point. I am using "persuasion evangelism" not only in the sense of strongly convincing someone that they should accept Christ, but also in bringing them along to responsible church membership.

The second reason I don't like the word "persuasion" very much is that to many it smacks of "manipulation." I want to distance myself as far from that as possible. I do not approve the use of unfair or fraudulent influence to make people Christians. Each unbeliever must be approached with the kind of Christian grace which allows him or her to maintain personal dignity, integrity and self-esteem.

However, with those reservations, I must say that for years I have searched for a suitable synonym and have not yet found one which satisfies me. So I continue to use "persuasion evangelism." One consolation is that persuasion is the English equivalent to the Greek *peitho*, and *peitho* is used frequently in the book of Acts to describe biblical evangelism.[5]

Some of my students have told me that they agree with 3-P evangelism, but that it does not go far enough. Many suggestions have been made for me to add a fourth

P or a fifth. For the purpose of defining evangelism as a basis for strategy planning, there is no other *P* to add. The three *P*s say it all. What my students have in mind is something beyond the definition of evangelism, namely additional elements which go into the evangelistic process. With that I agree. In fact, I like to list eight elements in the evangelistic cycle which should be conceptualized as moving in a circular fashion, never ending. They are: prayer, planning, power, presence, proclamation, persuasion, propagation, pedagogy and back to prayer.

_____ What About the Archbishops? _____

So far in this chapter on the meaning of evangelism I have not offered a concise, formal definition of evangelism. In some of my earlier writings I attempted to develop a new comprehensive definition of evangelism, but more recently I have given up on it. I have not been able to improve on what is known as "the archbishops' definition of evangelism." Formulated by a group of Anglican archbishops back in 1918, it states:

> To evangelize is so to present Christ Jesus in the power of the Holy Spirit, that men and women shall come to put their trust in God through Him, to accept Him as their Saviour, and serve Him as their King in the fellowship of His Church.

This is obviously a 3-P definition of evangelism. By it, evangelistic results are measured by how many people commit themselves to Jesus Christ and also to the Body of Christ, the Church.

Predictably, some, especially those who would defend

2-P evangelism, would disagree with the archbishops. One of these is J. I. Packer, the British theologian. He explains why he disagrees with the archbishops in his best-seller, *Evangelism and the Sovereignty of God.* He admits that the definition has much to commend it, but departs from them when they say that to evangelize is *so to do* something *that* something else will happen. He would prefer the definition to say that men and women *may* come rather than that men and women *shall* come. He faults the archbishops' statement by saying that "it defines evangelism in terms of an effect achieved in the lives of others; which amounts to saying that the essence of evangelizing is producing converts."[6]

What is J. I. Packer doing? Notice that he takes issue with the archbishops' definition precisely at the point where it constitutes itself a 3-P definition. Persuasion evangelism agrees with the archbishops that the essence of evangelizing is producing converts and ensuring that those converts end up in churches. Packer sees it otherwise. He argues that "The way to tell whether in fact you are evangelizing is not to ask whether conversions are known to have resulted from your witness. It is to ask whether you are faithfully making known the gospel message."[7] This is 2-P evangelism, as I have defined it.

In the Lausanne Congress on World Evangelization in 1974, John R. W. Stott brought up the archbishops' definition of evangelism in his plenary address, "The Biblical Basis of Evangelism." Then he quoted J. I. Packer, much as I have just done, and agreed with Packer. In the providence of God, both John Stott and I became charter members of the Lausanne Committee for World Evangelization. He was named chairperson of the Theology Working Group, and I was named chairperson of the Strategy Working Group. For years we carried on a friendly, but at times intense, dialogue on the definition of evangelism. He saw it as 2-P and I as 3-P.

Toward the end of the '70s the issue was resolved. John Stott himself proposed this definition of evangelism:

> The nature of evangelization is the communication of the Good News. The purpose of evangelization is to give individuals a valid opportunity to accept Jesus Christ. The goal of evangelization is the persuading of men and women to accept Jesus Christ as Lord and Savior, and serve Him in the fellowship of His Church.

The wording of that is such that it seems to satisfy the concerns of both 2-P and 3-P advocates. The Theology Working Group and the Strategy Working Group agreed, and it has become the operational definition of evangelism for the Lausanne Committee.

Either the Lausanne definition or the archbishops' definition of evangelism is an excellent basis for planning strategies of church growth. I lean toward the archbishops' because I am goal-oriented and I like the "so to . . . that." Others who may be more process-oriented prefer the Lausanne definition which omits that cause and effect relationship. Both of them relate evangelism to church growth.

NOTES

1. C. Peter Wagner, *Your Church Can Grow* (Ventura, CA: Regal Books, 1984), p. 14.
2. R. K. Orchard, *Missions in a Time of Testing* (London: Lutterworth Press, 1964), p. 92.
3. Colin Williams, *Faith in a Secular Age* (New York: Harper & Row Publishers, Inc., 1966), p. 12.
4. David B. Barrett, *World Christian Encyclopedia* (Oxford: Oxford University Press, 1982), p. 199.
5. See, for example, Acts 13:43; 17:4; 18:4; 26:28; 28:23-24.
6. J. I. Packer, *Evangelism and the Sovereignty of God* (Downer's Grove, Intervarsity Press, 1961), p. 40.
7. Ibid., p. 41.

7

Body Evangelism Helps
Grow Churches

The last two chapters on the meaning of mission and evangelism have been largely theoretical. In contrast, this chapter is mostly empirical. I have been arguing as strongly as I know how that the decisions one takes as to the definitions of mission and evangelism as a basis for planning strategy will make a difference out there on the field. Now I want to show how much a difference it actually can make.

When I was first introduced to the Church Growth Movement by Donald McGavran back in 1967, I was an active field missionary. Ever since then, I have been interested in researching the outcomes of different approaches to evangelism in terms of the growth of the churches involved in the programs. At that time I had just come through a year-long Evangelism in Depth effort which was held in Bolivia in 1965. In the '70s I was associated with Vergil Gerber in experimenting with what I like to call "body evangelism." Now in the '80s programs like James Montgomery's DAWN (Discipling a Whole Nation) program have emerged as more advanced developments in the evolution of a conscious relating of evangelism to church growth. My purpose in this chapter is to describe that evolution.

_____ **Three Streams of Evangelism** _____

While evangelicals tend to prioritize the evangelistic mandate, the methodologies developed for implementing it vary considerably. Most denominational headquarters staffs periodically promote a new evangelistic program and publish the resources to accompany it. Some of these are very good programs and benefit churches which use them greatly. Many parachurch organizations design programs to facilitate evangelism and market them to churches across denominational lines. Scores of such evangelistic methodologies exist.

When I speak of three streams of evangelism, I am not referring to these specific kinds of programs. I am looking back at the history of broad evangelistic moods which, since World War II, have had a substantial influence on how strategies for evangelism and church growth have been planned. In my own analysis I see the three streams as (1) crusade evangelism, (2) saturation evangelism and (3) body evangelism. I do not see them as fads which come and go. Rather, each one enjoyed a decade of great popularity, but each one continues strongly to the present time and I would expect them to continue indefinitely. Let's examine them one at a time.

Crusade Evangelism

While crusade evangelism brings memories of Dwight L. Moody, Reuben A. Torrey, Billy Sunday and many others, in modern times it gained considerable popularity with Billy Graham's famous Los Angeles crusade of 1949. It was Randolph Hearst's two-word telegram to his newspapers, "PUFF GRAHAM" which triggered the media and catapulted Billy Graham to celebrity status almost overnight. While God has raised up many evangelists who function well in a crusade-type setting, Billy Graham is the best known of them.

Holding evangelistic crusades was considered by many in the decade of the '50s as evangelism par excellence. And it has by no means ceased. Billy Graham himself has sponsored two international congresses for itinerant evangelists in Amsterdam with several thousand attending each one.

The usual way for a crusade to develop is for a number of churches in a metropolitan area to get together and invite a big-name evangelist. Under the general supervision of the evangelist's association, committees are organized, prayer chains are formed, a choir is recruited, counselors are trained in personal witnessing, the media is enlisted at all levels, cooperating churches are sought, funds are raised and a public arena is leased for the occasion. The excitement builds in the community, hopefully peaking when the professional evangelist arrives to preach for a given number of nights.

After each sermon an invitation is given for people to accept Jesus Christ as their Saviour. In some crusades the evangelist also gives a secondary invitation to Christians to rededicate their lives to God. Those who respond are asked to come forward where they are met one-on-one by those who have been trained as crusade counselors. After the interview, the counselor prays with the inquirer either for salvation or rededication. Then the person making the decision records it on a card with their name and address. If they have a church preference, they are asked to indicate that also.

Following the crusade, and in some cases after each meeting, the decision cards are distributed equitably among the cooperating churches. The evangelist moves on, leaving the follow-up to those who received the cards. Some evangelistic associations mail material such as Bible correspondence courses, literature written by the evangelist or magazines to the inquirers as an aid to follow-up.

The evangelist or the evangelistic association then reports the results of the crusade to its constituency. These are Christian men and women who have been praying for the evangelist and who have been contributing financially to the ministry. They are anxious to know whether the crusade they have been supporting was successful. Almost invariably, the reports say, yes, the crusade was successful. The information provided to back that up registers how many persons attended the crusade and how many inquirers responded. It is only very rarely, if at all, that an evangelistic association will provide any information relating to whether the crusade helped the cooperating churches grow.

Perhaps this is beginning to change. One of the finest new books on crusade evangelism comes from Sterling W. Huston who directs the North American crusades for the Billy Graham Evangelistic Association. Its title: *Crusade Evangelism and the Local Church.* I for one was delighted to see that Sterling Huston accepts both the archbishops' definition and the Lausanne Committee working definition, mentioned in the last chapter, as valid definitions of evangelism. He comments, "These definitions strongly affirm that a key objective of effective evangelism is 'disciples' who demonstrate their commitment to Christ by their commitment to a local body of believers."[1]

Here is a fresh, new emphasis in a milieu traditionally dominated by a proclamation evangelism emphasis. In all fairness, we note that this emphasis has not been absent from Billy Graham's own thinking. Back in 1966 at the Berlin World Congress on Evangelism, Billy Graham said, "It seems to me that we cannot improve on the definition of evangelism that was given to us by the Archbishops' Committee on Evangelism in 1918."[2]

Accepting a 3-P definition of evangelism is a commendable first step. Reporting the success or failure of each crusade in terms of how many disciples are made yet remains on the agenda. I fear that not too many crusade evangelists will be willing to do it. For one thing, it would involve their staffs in research which would be both expensive and time consuming. For another, some evangelists, certainly not all, might be threatened by the possibility that the results of a given crusade, in terms of subsequent church growth, might turn out to be minimal. This could be discouraging to their supporters.

Sterling Huston has made a commendable start in doing this in the book just referred to. He mentions, for example, the Cincinnati crusade of 1977 in which 83 percent of the inquirers said they were attending church regularly after five weeks. In Sydney, Australia, an estimated 70 percent were attending church a year later. In neither one of these reports, however, are new converts and rededicated Christians distinguished from one another. But in the London Harringay crusade of 1954, 64 percent of the outsiders who made decisions were said to be involved in churches a year later.[3]

Some crusades have had a positive effect on whole denominations or regions. The Tommy Hicks crusade in Buenos Aires in 1954 caused accelerated growth in several denominations, notably the Assemblies of God. The denomination had been losing membership before the crusade, and was down to 174 members. But by 1956, two years after the crusade, they counted 2,000 members. Church growth researcher Arno W. Enns sees a cause-and-effect relationship.[4]

Another dramatic change in growth rates came in Kampuchea (then called Cambodia) when Stanley Mooneyham held successive crusades in April and November 1971. At that time the national church, affiliated with the Christian and Missionary Alliance, had grown to 600 members through many years. Membership was up to 1,000 a year later and reached 5,000 before the Communists took over.

These are some of the positive cases. My continuing research on this matter shows that a considerable number of crusades cannot claim such results. So as not to cause embarrassment, I will not mention names of evangelists or even cities, but suffice it to say that many crusades will show 10 percent or less of those who made first-time decisions becoming involved in a local church one year after the crusade. In some of the reports even the researchers are not sure. I have a research report of a particular crusade which showed 7 percent of first-time decisions in churches. Then after that appeared, the evangelistic association itself sponsored a follow-up research project and came up with a figure of 16 percent.

Saturation Evangelism

During the banner decade of the '50s the most prominent crusade evangelist in Latin America was Harry Strachan, founder of the Latin America Mission. His son, Kenneth, graduated from Wheaton College and returned to become his father's crusade manager, helping him organize meetings in the major cities. Kenneth Strachan was a restless man with an inquisitive intellect. He began to notice that while they were seeing large crowds gather for the crusades and a large number of people making decisions for Christ, when he went back to the same cities a year or two later, relatively few of those who made decisions had become responsible church members. Both he and his father had hoped that their fruit would be fruit that remains, but it did not appear that such was the case.

This discovery disturbed Kenneth Strachan so much that he took a leave of absence from his regular ministry. He spent a year researching three of the most rapidly growing movements in Latin America: the Communists, the Jehovah's Witnesses and the Pentecostals. His studies led him to the conclusion that the basic defect of his father's crusade evangelism was the excessive emphasis on the ministry of the outside evangelist and not enough emphasis on the mobilization of the believers in the existing churches for continuous evangelism. He didn't use the term, but he discovered what I like to call the "follow-up gap." That is the discrepancy between the total number of inquirers who make first-time decisions for Christ and the number of them who end up in churches.

Over a period of time, Kenneth Strachan developed a new kind of program designed to close the follow-up gap. He called it Evangelism in Depth, but later the term "saturation evangelism" was applied to it by missiologist George Peters, then teaching at Dallas Theological Seminary.[5] Instead of operating in one city as did most crusades, Strachan projected Evangelism in Depth for a whole nation. Instead of a couple of weeks, it lasted a whole year. Instead of one crusade, it employed many crusades on local church, city, regional and national levels. But its key innovation was the attempt to train every believer in every church to be an active and continuous propagator of the faith. It began in Nicaragua in 1960 and

operated in 11 Latin American nations during that decade.
The model was copied in many other countries such as
New Life for All and Christ for All in Africa, Total Mobilization in Japan, Evangelism Deep and Wide in Vietnam,
Christ the Only Way in the Philippines and many others. In
the U.S.A. regional saturation evangelism programs were
carried out in Appalachia and Eastern Pennsylvania, and in
a national effort called Key '73.

I myself participated in the year-long Evangelism in
Depth movement in Bolivia in 1965, where I was a missionary. It was the largest and best organized national
movement I had seen in my entire missionary career. I
was impressed by the multiplication of prayer cells, by the
national radio broadcasts on both long- and shortwave, by
the well-organized steering committees, by the personnel
sent to Bolivia from the Latin America Mission in Costa
Rica, by the newspaper *En Marcha,* by the parades
through the streets, by the media attention previously
unknown, by the special campaigns for women and
Aymara Indians and children and university students, by
the large pastors' conference, by the huge crusades, and
most of all by the number of decisions for Christ during the
year. At the time the total evangelical community in
Bolivia numbered about 60,000. During Evangelism in
Depth, 20,000 decisions for Christ were recorded.

To say the least, I was highly enthusiastic about Evangelism in Depth when I came to Fuller to study church
growth under Donald McGavran in 1967. While I was in
the process of writing my thesis on the Protestant movement in Bolivia, my mentor, Ralph Winter, suggested I
build in a study of Evangelism in Depth. My assignment
was to try to discover how it had affected the growth of
churches. I was greatly surprised to discover that the
year-long program had not increased the rate of growth of

the churches. In fact the percentage of annual growth of the seven cooperating denominations for which reasonably accurate statistics were available was greater for the year just preceding Evangelism in Depth than it was either during 1964 or during the two following years.

Careful projections on a logarithmic graph indicate that the total membership of the seven participating denominations was 27,676 in 1967, two years after Evangelism in Depth. But if those same denominations had continued to grow at the rate they were enjoying just previous in Evangelism in Depth, they should have totaled about 32,000 in 1967.[6]

Research done by George W. Peters on Evangelism in Depth in Costa Rica, Guatemala, Venezuela and Bolivia revealed a similar phenomenon. He applauds the large number of professions of faith during the efforts. But he is baffled "that a comparable rise in figures cannot be shown in church membership."[7] Paul Enyart found that the Friends churches in Guatemala lost members during Evangelism in Depth and continued to lose for several years following the effort.[8] Edward Murphy said that a study one year after Evangelism in Depth "reveals that the saturation effort has not yet produced an increase in numerical growth in the churches.[9] Studies by David Dyck in the Dominican Republic,[10] by Jerold Reed in Ecuador,[11] and by others reach the same conclusions.

This is not to say that Evangelism in Depth had no effect on church growth. Reports from many local congregations indicate that it did help them to grow. The Central America Mission churches in Ecuador gained many new members.[12] Almost universally, participants had a warm feeling about Evangelism in Depth. Nevertheless, the follow-up gap which Kenneth Strachan attempted to close remained open. Unfortunately Strachan died a premature death in 1965, or he himself might have done the research and adjusted his program accordingly. Positive adjustments have been made in some saturation evangelism designs, such as New Life for All, and they are showing good results.

Body Evangelism

Just about the time when serious questions were being raised about the lasting results of saturation evangelism, an unrelated event took place which God ultimately used to bring about a third stream of evangelism: body evangelism. The event was the publication in 1969 of the epochal study, *Latin American Church Growth,* by William R. Read, Victor M. Monterroso, and Harmon A. Johnson, done at Fuller Seminary under the supervision of Donald McGavran. Among the many revealing findings of the research was one particularly disturbing to those of us who were part of the Interdenominational Foreign Mission Association (IFMA) and the Evangelical Foreign Missions Association (EFMA). The study compared the number of missionaries deployed in Latin America to the number of resulting church members. Much to our surprise the IFMA/EFMA missionaries had the lowest ratio of church members to missionaries when compared to mainline conciliar missions, Seventh-Day Adventists and Pentecostals. While a full 42 percent of the missionaries in Latin America were IFMA/EFMA related, only 5 percent of the church members could be traced to their efforts. [13]

Fortunately for all concerned, the reaction of the leadership of the IFMA and EFMA to these rather startling findings was constructive. They called an emergency meeting of 50 of their executives from missions working in Latin America in Elburn, Illinois in 1970. They asked

Vergil Gerber, Executive Director of the Evangelical Missions Information Service (EMIS) and me to be co-chairpersons of the meeting. At the time I was still living in Bolivia and directing our mission.

As I recall those three or four days of meetings, I do not have positive memories. The executives were in somewhat of a surly mood. The morning Bible studies and prayer time led by Melvin Hodges of the Assemblies of God were a high point, but the rest of the sessions were little more than organized confusion. One of the chief points of debate was the relative value of the Church Growth Movement then taking shape at Fuller Seminary where Read, Monterroso and Johnson's research had been done. The cons seemed clearly to outweigh the pros. Since I myself had studied at Fuller under McGavran, I was called upon to answer many questions that I had no answers for. Mostly out of frustration, I believe, a closing mandate of the Elburn Consultation was that Vergil Gerber and Peter Wagner would somehow undertake the implementation of church growth principles in Latin America and report back to the rest.

Neither Gerber nor I had any sense of God's leading at the time. The only thing we knew to do was pray for God's guidance. I returned to Bolivia and Gerber to his office in Wheaton, not having any idea of what might be in store for the decade of the '70s. But God knew, and He showed it to us in His time.

———————— **The Bible Fellowship Church** ————————

In the fall of 1971, I responded to the call to join Donald McGavran on the faculty of the Fuller School of World Mission. Then early in 1972, I somewhat reluctantly accepted an unusual assignment. Our dean, Arthur F.

Glasser, had been scheduled to speak to the pastors of the Bible Fellowship Church, a denomination of some 40 or 50 churches centered in Eastern Pennsylvania and New Jersey, on the subject of church growth. He couldn't make it, so he asked me to go in his place.

Up to this time the entire Church Growth Movement had concentrated its research and teaching on the Third World. No models for teaching it to Americans and applying it to American churches had yet been developed. As the time approached I found myself with very few ideas as to how this seminar might take shape, and I was increasingly apprehensive about it. As I was praying, however, God impressed me to write to the denomination and ask for the membership statistics of their churches over the past 10 years. On the airplane I constructed a statistical chart of the growth history of each of their churches over the past 10 years. As a friend drove me to the conference I asked him to stop at a drug store where I purchased a couple of packages of simple graph paper. A format was beginning to take shape.

In the seminar itself I spent a day or so teaching basic church growth principles as well as I could to pastors of 46 local churches. Some thought it was helpful, others weren't so sure. Then I told them I wanted each of them to draw a 10-year graph of growth of their church and study it. I provided the graph paper and the necessary statistics. As they were drawing the graphs I began to detect a sense of excitement invading the room. Small conversations began here and there, and some "eureka" moments began to occur. The lines drawn across the paper were providing new information and insights about the churches they had been pastoring. Interest in the seminar began to increase.

When they finished we added up the total membership

of the 46 churches in 1961, 1966 and 1971. It came out to
be 4,500 for each date. The denomination was on a distinct
plateau. I then challenged each of them in prayer and faith
to extend their graph of growth for five years into the
future on the basis of how many new members they
believed they could trust God for. When these were added
up, the flat graph of growth took a sharp swing upward. So
far as I know, this was the first "faith projection" made in a
church growth seminar.

What were the results?

Daniel G. Ziegler, director of the Church Extension
Department of the Bible Fellowship Church, wrote a
report in early 1981 entitled, "How Did the B.F.C. Do in
the Seventies?" On the first page he refers to the faith
projections made in 1972. Then reports that in the '70s
"the membership of the Bible Fellowship Church rose by
1,205, the largest numerical increase in any decade of our
history." He then goes on to say, "But percentage growth
is a more accurate measure of comparison than raw
numerical increase. In the decade of the '70s the church
grew 26.5 percent. One would have to go back to the '30s
to find a higher percentage of growth . . . . The one decade, the '70s, outgrew the previous *three* decades by 777
members, a phenomenal 282 percent!"

———————— **The Venezuela Experiment** ————————

At the close of the seminar I, of course, had no idea
whether the participating churches would grow or not. But
I did have a deep sense of God's blessing, deep enough to
call Vergil Gerber and suggest that we might now have a
model developing as a follow-on to the Elburn Consultation. I asked Gerber if, through his EMIS network, he
might be able to identify a group of church leaders in Latin

America who would be willing to set up three church growth workshops, one year apart. The two of us would teach church growth principles to the pastors, challenge them to make faith projections, then return for two successive years to measure what had happened. He soon found a group in Venezuela which invited us to begin in June 1972. They represented churches affiliated with the Orinoco River Mission, the Evangelical Free Church, The Evangelical Alliance Mission, the Church of the Foursquare Gospel and the United World Mission.

The so-called "Venezuela Experiment" was encouraging. Fifty-two churches cooperated. Their growth rates for the 10 years previous to making faith projections was 60 percent DGR (decadal growth rate). The rate for the two years following the first workshop had risen to 250 percent. Notice that we are measuring the results in a 3-P category. We are measuring not how many people heard the gospel nor how many people made decisions for Christ, but how many new people actually became responsible church members.

Four important developments emerged from the Venezuela experiment:

1. *A model.* A model had been designed for a new type of evangelistic effort. This was based entirely on local resources, catalyzed into evangelistic action by outside consultants. It seemed to close the follow-up gap. When measured a year or two later, the cooperating churches by and large were still growing.

2. *A book.* Vergil Gerber made the model accessible by presenting it in a book, *God's Way to Keep a Church Going and Growing* (Regal Books). Known popularly as "The Gerber Manual," it went through five printings in English, and was translated and published in approximately 50 other languages. New translations continue to

appear. No other book that I know of has had such a wide-spread influence in making known the principles of church growth around the world.

3. *A person.* God called Vergil Gerber to give a large portion of his time during the '70s to conduct workshops on the Venezuela model for church leaders on all continents. Before poor health curtailed his ministry at the decade's end, he had taught in over 50 nations. Between 1973 and 1980, he logged approximately one workshop every six weeks. Few evangelical leaders, if any, have been as widely used of God to stimulate grass-roots, church-based evangelistic efforts which have produced fruit that remains.

4. *A term.* At the time of the Venezuela experiment, Ray Stedman's book, *Body Life* (Regal Books), was very popular. It dealt with how members of the Body of Christ were supposed to relate to one another biblically. Gerber and I thought that "body evangelism" would be a good companion term. It would highlight the kind of evangelism (3-P) which would insist on bringing unbelievers to faith in Christ and into the Body of Christ as a part of the evangelistic process itself. Thus it could be distinguished from crusade evangelism and saturation evangelism. The term never has become a household word among evangelicals, but I still think it has merit and I use it.

_____ Measuring the Results _____

Crusade evangelism and saturation evangelism traditionally measure their success in terms of how many hear the gospel through their efforts and how many inquirers register decisions for Christ. The evangelist or the team can immediately communicate these results to headquarters and they can be channeled into the media or sent out in letters to the supporters. This is an appealing feature of measuring evangelistic results on what we have called a 2-P pattern.

A disadvantage of body evangelism is that it cannot be measured so rapidly. Since we are dealing with the growth rates of cooperating churches, it takes time to observe them, usually two to five years. It requires more patience than most evangelists or evangelistic associations possess. Furthermore, many of those who are using the body evangelism model also lack the patience to check up diligently after every one of their efforts. If they don't, it is difficult to know when mid-course corrections need to be made in the strategy.

Here are some examples of results which have come in:

Lusaka, Zambia. Vergil Gerber always took team members with him when he did a workshop. In Lusaka in 1977, Waldron Scott was his companion. Here is Scott's report:

"As a result of the workshop, the Pilgrim Wesleyan Church got busy and updated all their statistics back to 1960, then they put them on graphs and showed them to their pastors. Their next step was to 'clean up' their rolls. They had over 2,000 people on their rolls. By the time they got finished with the cleaning-up exercise, the membership had dropped by 960! That was the end of 1975, six months after we had been with them. During the following year, 1976, however, they experienced a 40 percent increase in church membership over 1975! Already in 1977 the church membership has shown a great increase and they are now almost back to the original 2,000—except this time their figures are very firm and represent real, active church members."

Burundi, Africa. Donald Hohensee reports that the

World Gospel Church in Burundi had shown a 28 percent DGR (decadal growth rate) for the 10 years preceding the Gerber workshop of May 1974. At the workshop the participants made a bold faith projection of 285 percent for the next five years. At the end of the five-year period, the rate was actually 492 percent DGR.

Australia. Win C. Arn, an American church leader, became a student and later an advocate of church growth and its body evangelism corollary back in 1972. He subsequently founded the Institute for American Church Growth, and developed a workshop which, like Gerber's, features a faith projection exercise. In 1975 he presented his basic seminar to pastors and leaders from the Churches of Christ in all the states of Australia. He went back for an advanced seminar in 1976. According to Kevin Crawford, Director of Home Missions and Evangelism, the churches were losing membership at 1.3 percent per year when Arn first arrived. Afterwards the participating churches, those which made faith projections, enjoyed an average yearly growth rate of 14.5 percent, a total turnaround of 15.8 percent per year.

Rosario, Argentina. Perhaps the most publicized application of body evangelism took place in conjunction with more traditional crusade evangelism in Rosario in 1976. The Luis Palau Evangelistic Association is the only crusade-oriented organization so far which has experimented with the body evangelism model. Key to the planning were Edgardo Silvoso, Palau's brother-in-law; Vergil Gerber and Juan Carlos Miranda, now with the Fuller Institute of Evangelism and Church Growth. Previous to the execution of the "Rosario Plan" the participating churches were growing at a rate of 1.4 percent DGR. Seventeen months after the Luis Palau crusade the rate had gone up to over 1,000 percent DGR. The follow-up gap was narrowed also. Approximately 50 percent of those making first-time decisions ended up in churches.

Philippines. In 1974 a body evangelism workshop was held by Vergil Gerber and Donald McGavran in the Philippines. The complete report can be found in James H. Montgomery and Donald A. McGavran's *The Discipling of a Nation.*[14] Suffice it to say that four of the major cooperating denominations, the American Baptists, the Christian and Missionary Alliance, the Church of the Foursquare Gospel and the Southern Baptists had shown a 56 percent DGR for 10 years previous to the workshop. During the subsequent four years, the rate rose to 201 percent.

Reports such as these could be multiplied. While it is true that some attempts at body evangelism have fizzled, the general consensus of those who have been involved over the years is positive enough to suggest that it has an edge on more traditional models of crusade and saturation evangelism. Not that they are opposed to one another. Body evangelism principles can easily be incorporated into crusades or saturation-type programs.

NOTES

1. Sterling W. Huston, *Crusade Evangelism and the Local Church* (Minneapolis: World Wide, 1984), p. 114.
2. Billy Graham, "Why the Berlin Congress?" in *One Race, One Gospel, One Task,* ed. Carl F. Henry and W. Stanley Mooneyham (Minneapolis: World Wide Publications, 1967), 1:25.
3. Sterling W. Huston, *Crusade Evangelism and the Local Church,* pp. 141-42; 147-48.
4. Arno W. Enns, *Man, Milieu and Mission in Argentina* (Grand Rapids: Wm. B. Eerdmans Publishing Co., 1971), pp. 79-81.
5. George W. Peters, *Saturation Evangelism* (Grand Rapids: Zondervan Publishing House, 1970).
6. C. Peter Wagner, *The Protestant Movement in Bolivia* (Pasadena: Wm. Carey Library, 1970), pp. 164-75.

7. Peters, *Saturation Evangelism,* p. 74.

8. Paul Enyart, *Friends in Central America* (Pasadena: Wm. Carey Library, 1970), pp. 60, 137.

9. Edward F. Murphy, "Follow Through Evangelism in Latin America" in *Mobilizing for Saturation Evangelism,* ed. Clyde W. Taylor and Wade T. Coggins (Wheaton: Evangelical Missions Information Service, 1970), p. 184.

10. David W. Dyck, "The Missionary Church in the Dominican Republic" (M.A. project, Fuller School of World Mission, 1975).

11. Jerold F. Reed, "A Componential Analysis of the Ecuadorian Protestant Church" (D.Miss. dissertation, Fuller Seminary School of World Mission, 1974), p. 93.

12. William R. Read, Victor M. Monterroso and Harmon Johnson, *Latin American Church Growth* (Grand Rapids: Wm. B. Eerdmans Publishing Co., 1969), p. 161.

13. Ibid., p. 57.

14. James H. Montgomery and Donald A. McGavran, *The Discipling of a Nation* (Global Church Growth Bulletin, 1980).

8
Getting Off on the Right Track

The last two chapters have dealt with the theoretical and the practical sides of evangelism respectively. Theoretically, the most appropriate way to define evangelism, if it is to relate to strategies for church growth, is to think of it as persuasion: bringing unbelievers to faith in Jesus Christ and also responsible church membership. I call it 3-P evangelism because it includes not only presence and proclamation, but moves on to persuasion.

In an attempt to apply 3-P evangelism to actual field situations, I have used the term "body evangelism." The last chapter describes how body evangelism differs from traditional approaches such as crusade evangelism and saturation evangelism and it reports some of the practical outcomes from the field. Generally speaking, the body evangelism approach produces more satisfactory results when measured by increases in the rates of growth of the participating churches. So if one is to develop strategies geared specifically to church growth, body evangelism is a highly appropriate way of going about it.

But a question remains: Exactly what characteristics of body evangelism stimulate greater church growth than the more traditional approaches to evangelism? I believe that the most important characteristic has already been described: the choice of a 3-P definition of evangelism. While at times we poke fun at "theory," we know down deep that theory determines practice. What we do depends a great deal on what we think. Most crusade and saturation evangelism programs are based on a 2-P definition of evangelism. They measure their results in terms of how many hear and understand the gospel. The bottom line for 3-P evangelism involves a dual commitment: to Christ and also to the Body of Christ. This is how it ties into church growth.

If the question of definition has been settled, the first step has been taken toward getting off on the right track toward effective strategies for church growth. But several other characteristics of body evangelism need to be considered in planning strategy. The purpose of this chapter is to summarize these in a practical and useful way.

Goal Setting

When I described body evangelism previously, I purposely mentioned the concept of "faith projections" several times. Making faith projections is one way of setting goals. Specifically, body evangelism encourages two kinds of faith projections: (1) *expansion growth,* that is increase in membership in a given local congregation and (2) *extension growth,* that is planting new churches.

The recommended planning scope for faith projections is five years. But for good strategy planning, the faith projection should be renewed ideally every year or at least every two years. In this way you are constantly keeping track of what God is doing and can better tune in to what you believe He will be doing in the near future. A step-by-step, fill-in-the-blanks, 40-page practical resource for guiding church leaders in making faith projections is *The Church Growth Survey Handbook* compiled by Bob Waymire and myself. Waymire is an engineer and he contributes that expertise to the development of church growth strategies. Anyone who wishes to make use of the principles I am describing in this book, should have *The Church Growth Survey Handbook* as a tool.[1]

The crucial importance of goal setting has become increasingly clear as church growth strategies have been applied worldwide. For example, after Vergil Gerber held body evangelism workshops in Central America and featured faith projections, the churches which made them began to grow. Malon Collins of the Central America Mission wrote enthusiastically to Gerber some years later and said: "Your emphasis in Honduras three or four years ago on promoting church growth through the establishing of goals has been one of the primary causes of growth on all our fields. Leaders in El Salvador, Honduras and Nicaragua have accepted those principles and implemented them with varying degrees of enthusiasm." Collins then goes on to make this significant statement: "Most of the growth has taken place where it was planned."

In the United States, an influential Church Growth Center has been established in Corunna, Indiana by Kent Hunter. For several years, Hunter has been applying the principles I am describing as a consultant to hundreds of churches. He is one of the few church growth consultants who takes pains to measure the outcome of his efforts in rates of church growth. He worked with the Missouri District of the Lutheran Church Missouri Synod for several years, helping them, among other things, to understand the value of faith projections in planning their growth strategy. The churches in the district which made faith projections increased membership by 17.7 percent between 1980 and 1984, while the membership of the churches which did not participate decreased by 1.2 percent. In participating churches worship attendance increased 3 percent while it decreased 1.8 percent in nonparticipating churches.

What is the rationale behind this phenomenon? I see goal setting as biblical, as natural and as practical.

1. *Goal setting is biblical.* Properly understood, goal setting can be seen as a modern expression of the biblical concept of faith. Faith, in the biblical context, is multidimensional. There is a kind of faith which we could call "saving faith." Ephesians 2:8 says, "For by grace you have been saved through faith." Then another kind of faith can be called "sanctifying faith." This is the kind of faith described as a fruit of the Spirit in Galatians 5:22. I like to call a third kind of faith "possibility thinking faith," naming it after the book title *Moving Ahead with Possibility Thinking* by Robert Schuller. Schuller, a long-time friend, has taught me a great deal about believing God for great things in the future. During the years of rapid growth in his church in Garden Grove, California, now called the Crystal Cathedral, Schuller practiced body evangelism although he did not use the term.

Possibility thinking faith is the faith of Hebrews 11:1: "Now faith is the substance of things hoped for, the evidence of things not seen." Notice that nothing past or present is hoped for. Things hoped for are future. Putting substance on something future is called goal setting. One way of doing it is to tune in to God, ask Him what His purpose for your church is over the next five years, then plot it on graph paper. This is making a faith projection. I agree with Edward Dayton that "every goal is a statement of faith."

Exercising faith seems to tap into a source of divine power which is not ordinarily released in other ways. I do not as yet understand all of the theology behind this except that the Bible teaches "without faith it is impossible to please Him" (Heb. 11:6). An increasing amount of field data suggests that the principle works. I realize that some Christian leaders criticize goal setting as an approach which is more carnal than spiritual. And I share their concern, because goal setting can be used for sinful motives. But I do not believe it has to be this way. I believe that a faith projection can be a significant spiritual exercise which is pleasing to God.

2. *Goal setting is natural.* There seems to be something in human nature which is activated by goal setting with no reference to whether a person is a Christian or not. One of the scientists who has brought this to public attention is Maxwell Maltz in his popular book, *Psycho-Cybernetics.* Maltz says:

> There is an abundance of scientific evidence which shows that the human brain and nervous system operate purposefully in accordance with the known principles of Cybernetics to accomplish goals of the individual. Insofar as function is concerned, the brain and nervous system constitute a marvelous and complex "goal striving mechanism," a sort of built-in automatic guidance system which works *for* you as a "success mechanism," or *against* you as a "failure mechanism," depending on how "YOU," the operator, operate it and the goals you set for it.[2]

It is not my purpose here to review Maltz' evidence for his conclusion. But, reflecting theologically, it seems that if what he finds is true it may well be something that God intended for human beings in creation. I would think that this "goal striving mechanism" has been designed by God, although I do not know how to prove it. If it is, that makes it easier to understand why making faith projections turns out to help churches grow.

3. *Goal setting is practical.* Examples abound of how making faith projections has actually accelerated church growth. Of all nationalities, Filipinos seem to be as enthusiastic about goal setting as any other. They also have a special ability to attach motivational slogans to their faith projections. For instance, the Philippine Christian and Missionary Alliance is operating under "Target 2-2-2." They are trusting God to increase their total of baptized members to 2 million and the number of organized churches to 20,000 by the year 2000. These are very high numbers, but they are confident that it can be done. They have already successfully completed their "Target 400" and their "Target 100 Thousand" efforts. These past faith projections have brought the average annual growth rate of both membership and churches to an amazing 20 percent so that they can expect to grow over 500 percent per decade.

The Conservative Baptists in the Philippines call their program "H-20-T," the Foursquare "Five Til 85," the Association of Bible Churches "Expansion 100," The Baptist Conference of the Philippines "Objective Ten Thousand," and the Church of the Nazarene "Strive By Five." The Nazarenes, incidentally, grew from 2,537 members in 1974 to 6,797 in 1981. And their churches multiplied from 41 to 106. Little wonder that the Philippines is currently one of the world's flash points of church growth.

Another flash point of growth is Korea. The Yoido Full Gospel Church in Seoul has become the world's largest with over 500,000 members. Its pastor, my good friend Paul Yonggi Cho, believes in goal setting. I recall that when I first met him in 1976 his church had only 50,000 members or so. At that time he told me his goal was a half million by 1984, the hundredth anniversary of Protestantism in Korea. Lack of adequate facilities threw his faith projection off by a few months, but God had given him the half million by 1985.

One of Cho's fine books on church growth is entitled *Successful Home Cell Groups.* In the last chapter, he says he wants to "show how to put it all together so you will have church growth unlimited." He frequently gets questions from pastors who want principles which will help their churches grow like Cho's. His response? "The number-one requirement for having real church growth—unlimited church growth—is to set goals."[3] Pastors like Cho have found that goal setting is indeed practical.

Research

One of the secrets of intelligent goal setting is research. The most exhaustive treatment on how to go about this research is found in Edward Dayton and David Fraser's *Planning Strategies for World Evangelization.*[4] Their work is geared toward what we usually think of as missionary work. Another resource, condensed and simplified and geared toward church growth itself, is *The Church Growth Survey Handbook,* mentioned previously.

At least three kinds of research will be helpful as a basis for planning strategies for church growth: (1) preliminary research, (2) diagnostic research and (3) evaluative research.

1. *Preliminary research.* In the early stages of strategy planning, it is important to define the target. Invari-

ably, multiple options for outreach ministry appear, so there must be some basis on which to sort them out and assign priorities. Preliminary research deals essentially with testing the soil, to use the agricultural analogy. Chapter 4 describes the soil-testing process in detail. In a subsequent chapter, I will discuss some practical ways to identify targets for outreach. Not much more then, needs to be said at this point about preliminary research. But we do need to include it on this list, so it will not be neglected. It is a very important consideration in making faith projections. If the target is a group at -3 on the resistance-receptivity axis the faith projection will be different from a group at +5 on the axis.

2. *Diagnostic research.* Diagnostic research attempts to answer two questions about the recent past in a given church or cluster of churches. First, what has been happening? Secondly, why has it been happening?

The "what" is answered by studying growth rates over the past 10 years. Much experience has indicated that 10 years is a useful diagnostic period. History older than 10 years may have some nostalgic value and may be fascinating to a few, but it has minimal value for diagnosis. Sometimes a period of less than 10 years is used, obviously for a church which is under 10 years of age, but also for churches which may show a radical change in growth history sometime between three and 10 years in the past. Still, if the church is old enough, the 10-year period is recommended.

The first step in diagnosis is to gather the necessary data. The ideal diagnostic information is composite membership. This is a yearly average of church membership at year's end, and both worship attendance and Sunday School attendance averaged over the year. If it is not possible to obtain all three pieces of information, diagnosis can be done with one or two of them, although not as well as with all three. Note that Sunday School attendance is most useful for churches which have strong adult as well as children's programs in the Sunday School. If a given Sunday School is, to all intents and purposes, children only, I suggest skipping this category.

The data need to be gathered for a 10-year period. This means that 11 pieces of data are needed, a fact which often escapes the attention of some. This information should be placed on a chart. Then growth rates are calculated. Annual growth rates (AGR) should be figured for each of the 10 years of the diagnostic period. Also a decadal growth rate (DGR) should be calculated for the entire 10-year period. The AGR and the DGR are the standard measurements used. Some church growth researchers also use the AAGR, which means average annual growth rate. It provides the same information as the DGR, and whether or not to use it is largely a matter of personal preference.

For a 10-year diagnostic period, the AGRs and the DGR are simple to calculate. However, calculating the DGR for a period other than 10 years (or calculating any AAGR) is another matter. It is a very useful thing to do in many diagnostic situations, but it requires a mathematical sophistication above that of most church and mission leaders. Because of this, *The Church Growth Survey Handbook* has simplified it and brought it within the grasp of most people. The handbook shows how to make these calculations either by using charts provided or by using a scientific calculator which has the y^x (or x^y) and $1/x$ and $=$ functions.

As points of comparison, it has been found that varying DGRs can be described as follows:

25 percent DGR—marginal growth
50 percent DGR—fair growth
100 percent DGR—good growth
200 percent DGR—excellent growth
300 percent DGR—outstanding growth
500 percent DGR—incredible growth

It may seem surprising, but many churches in America and other parts of the world are sustaining a 500 percent DGR or more. Some are in the thousands. Even some denominations as a whole are increasing at that rate, notably some of the younger, first generation groups. For example, the Philippine Christian and Missionary Alliance I mentioned previously is growing at over 500 percent DGR. But while this is so, it is relatively rare. A DGR of 100 percent is considered very healthy both for a local church and even more so for a denomination, wherever it may be located.

When you have the data and the growth rates, graphs of growth should be drawn. Here is where *The Church Growth Survey Handbook* is also useful because it has blank graphs ready to use, along with permission to photocopy them in any quantity. Two kinds of graphs are recommended: a bar graph showing the annual growth rate (AGRs) and a line graph showing membership or composite membership over the 10 years.

Studying this information will provide you with the "what" of the diagnostic period. In many cases valuable information is immediately provided by this simple procedure, information which may even come as a surprise to those who have been close to the work being studied for years.

But graphs of growth often raise more questions than they answer. They tell "what" but not "why." The whys of church growth become more evident the more the researcher has what are frequently called "church growth eyes." Helping to provide these church growth eyes is the major task of the Church Growth Movement, and a considerable amount of literature as well as many academic and nonacademic training opportunities are available for this.

3. *Evaluative research.* Preliminary research and diagnostic research are called for prior to setting goals. But once the goals are set, and the process under way for reaching them, evaluative research comes into action. We recommend five-year goals for growth. But just because the goals are set does not mean that they will automatically be accomplished. Something can, and often does, go wrong. Unforeseen circumstances can arise in much less than five years. This is why constant monitoring is necessary. As I have said before, I recommend that new five-year goals be set on an annual basis. This builds in the evaluative research necessary to know when things are going well and when they are not.

As part of this process, healthy pragmatism needs to be applied. Chapter one argues that Christian pragmatism need not be carnal, as is so much pragmatism of the world, but that it can be consecrated to the service of God. If a given method is not contributing to meeting the goals, substitute one which will. A certain ruthlessness is helpful when this needs to be done in order to counterbalance the excessive sentimentalism which so often dominates our attitudes toward things done in the church. People are important and feelings are important, but in order to prevent some people from obstructing the broader work of God, feelings at times have to be hurt. The Apostle Paul dismissed young John Mark, hurting not only his feelings but also the feelings of his colleague, Barnabas (see Acts

15:37-39). Discernment as to when this must be done is essential, and evaluative research will help us to gain discernment.

_____ **The Medical Model** _____

One of the analogies found very helpful for this part of the diagnostic process is the medical model. Biblically, the church is frequently referred to as the Body of Christ (see Eph. 1:22-23). Different parts of that spiritual Body such as head, joints, feet, hands, ears and eyes are mentioned. It is presumed that the Body of Christ, just as human bodies, can be sick or it can be well. The very use of the term "diagnostic research" reflects an assumption that the church can be approached with medical like tools. Several church growth researchers, myself included, have set out to identify the factors contributing to the health, good or bad, of the church. I first made an attempt at identifying the vital signs of a healthy church, then I concentrated on the church diseases which commonly obstruct growth.

I published the vital signs in 1976 in a book called *Your Church Can Grow: Seven Vital Signs of a Healthy Church.*[5] The book has circulated quite widely and has stimulated some additional research. I am personally aware of several projects done in graduate schools, some using computerized regression analysis techniques, to test the vital signs on empirical situations. One of these, a test on the British Baptist churches, was published in book form by Paul Beasley-Murray.[6] Generally speaking, the validity of the vital signs has been confirmed by the testing. While some of the tests on some of the signs have been inconclusive, none has been invalidated. Details on the vital signs are available in *Your Church Can Grow,* so I will simply list them here with a minimum of comment.

1. *A pastor who is a possibility thinker and whose dynamic leadership has been used to catalyze the entire church into action for growth.* Further research is turning up increasing evidence that the pastor is indeed the first vital sign of a healthy church. What the characteristics of a church growth pastor are turning out to be are summarized in one of my later books, *Leading Your Church to Growth.*[7]

2. *A well-mobilized laity which has discovered, has developed and is using all the spiritual gifts for growth.* The church growth pastor is essentially an equipper, that is, a person who is a leader, who sets goals for the church according to the will of God, and who motivates and mobilizes the lay people of the church for the kinds of ministry necessary to accomplish the goals. The key to the role of the laity is ministry through God-given spiritual gifts. A practical treatment of this can be found in my book *Your Spiritual Gifts Can Help Your Church Grow.*[8]

3. *A church big enough to provide the range of services that meet the needs and expectations of its members.* I have found no optimum size for a church. Depending on their philosophy of ministry, churches of almost any size can be the "proper size." Nevertheless, the rule of thumb is that the larger the church, the more specialized services it is able to provide to meet the needs of its members or potential members.

4. *The proper balance of the dynamic relationship between celebration, congregation and cell.* One of the most common felt needs among Christians is for fellowship or *koinonia*. The way this is managed can make a substantial difference as to whether the church remains a single cell under 200 members or breaks through the "200 barrier." It also is a reason for plateauing in larger churches.

5. *A membership drawn primarily from one homogene-*

ous unit. No one church can meet everyone's needs, so it is often helpful to concentrate on one segment of society and develop a ministry geared to the particular needs of that group. By no means, however, should this be used as an excuse for racism or discrimination.

6. *Evangelistic methods that have proved to make disciples.* I have elaborated on this in the previous chapter on body evangelism.

7. *Priorities arranged in biblical order.* I have elaborated on this in chapter 5, "The Meaning of Mission."

The negative side of the same coin exposes the diseases which can and do obstruct church growth. I have identified eight of these and published them in *Your Church Can Be Healthy.*[9] I hasten to say that this is not an attempt to describe all the diseases a church can get, but specifically those known to inhibit growth. My studies were done on Anglo-American churches, so I do not know if any or all of the diseases apply to churches of other cultures. My colleague, Eddie Gibbs, has applied them to British churches and come up with 13 diseases.[10] Again, details of the diseases can be found elsewhere, so I will describe them in very brief terms.

1. *Ethnikitis.* Ethnikitis is produced by a changing community usually in an urban area. It is one of the two terminal illnesses on the list and by far the greatest killer of churches in America.

2. *Ghost town disease.* Formerly called "old age," ghost town disease is caused by a disintegrating community, usually in rural areas. It is the other terminal illness on the list.

3. *People-blindness.* People-blindness is the malady which prevents the leaders of a church from seeing the significant cultural differences which separate people into groups, differences which tend to obstruct the communi-

cation of the gospel message. Lack of cultural sensitivity can be a detriment to growth, especially in pluralistic societies.

4. *Hypercooperativism.* A mistaken assumption is that the more churches cooperate with each other in evangelistic efforts, the more evangelism will get done. This has all too often not been the case, although good efforts are being made to avoid some mistakes of the past and improve the effect of area-wide evangelism on the growth of participating churches.

5. *Koinonitis.* The biblical concept of *koinonia* (fellowship) is a good thing, but if overdone it can stop church growth. "Fellowship inflammation" occurs when the people in a church become so concerned for the welfare of one another that they lose their vision for outsiders yet to believe. "Fellowship saturation" has strictly to do with the numbers of people in each fellowship group. There are known rules of thumb which need to be applied if this is a problem.

6. *Sociological strangulation.* This is the only disease on the list specific to growing churches. It occurs when the volume of people-flow exceeds the ability of the physical facilities to handle it. In American churches the two most immediate problem areas are sanctuary size and parking space.

7. *Arrested spiritual development.* When church members fail to mature in their spiritual lives, church growth will ordinarily suffer. Religious vitality cannot be maintained among groups of people who operate at low levels of faith, biblical knowledge, doctrinal conviction, prayer and morality. Church renewal is one of the cures for arrested spiritual development, and at this point the renewal movement and the Church Growth Movement intersect.

8. *Saint John's Syndrome.* This name is borrowed from the person who wrote about the disease in the Bible. John described it in chapters 2 and 3 of the book of Revelation. It is a disease of second-generation churches which lack the commitment of the first generation.

Understanding the vital signs and the growth-obstructing diseases is an important step toward discovering why the graphs of growth move up and down the way they do. This is diagnostic research that provides a very useful base on which to make informed faith projections for growth. The more you know about the recent past, the more realistic you can be in setting goals. One resource designed to aid pastors in diagnosing the health of their total congregation is called *Your Church Can Be Healthy,* available from the Charles E. Fuller Institute (Dept. 352-230, P.O. Box 91990, Pasadena, CA 91109-1990).

_____ **Planting New Churches** _____

Unlike the traditional models of crusade evangelism and saturation evangelism, body evangelism builds in setting goals for multiplying churches. *The Church Growth Survey Handbook* has graphs for doing diagnostic research and making faith projections for numbers of churches as well as for membership in a given local congregation. In all of Vergil Gerber's pioneering workshops, planting new churches was highlighted, as it is now in the second generation of body evangelism, Discipling a Whole Nation (DAWN).

Experience has taught me that it is dangerous to make categorical statements when dealing with church growth principles. But there is one which I have made frequently and will probably continue to make: *Planting new churches is the most effective evangelistic methodology known under heaven.* This is true on both new ground and old ground. New ground is out where no churches are now, such as in parts of Thailand or Indonesia or Niger. Few people dispute the need for multiplying churches on the frontiers. But old ground, places like Germany or the United States or Colombia where Christianity has been present for centuries, also needs new churches for evangelistic effectiveness. I believe that we must make every effort possible to renew existing churches, simultaneously multiplying new churches.

I have given several examples of vigorous growth as a result of applying principles of body evangelism. In every one of these, whether it be Zambia or Burundi or Central America or the Philippines or Venezuela, most of the new growth came from planting new churches. In Venezuela, for instance, the leaders of the churches affiliated with the work of the Orinoco River Mission reported two new churches in the previous five years. During the workshop their faith was built and they made a bold faith projection for 14 new churches over the next five years. Then they came back to the second workshop with smiles on their faces. In that one year they had actually planted 19 new churches! Their only problem previous to that was that they had forgotten that they should and could do it.

Since church planting is such an important part of planning strategies for church growth, it is regrettable that it must be given such a brief treatment in this book. But there is so much to say about it that a separate book would be required. There is a fine bibliography on church planting at the present time and new books are coming out regularly. The two I most recommend to my students for monocultural church planting at the present time are Charles Chaney's *Church Planting at the End of the Twentieth Century*[11] and Elmer Towns's *Getting a Church*

Started..[12] For cross-cultural church planting I recommend
David Hesselgrave's *Planting Churches Cross-Culturally*[13]
and Jerry Appleby's *Missions Have Come Home to America.*[14] I myself teach extensively on church planting both in
the classroom and in seminars. My lectures on the subject
are now available in a self-study resource *How to Plant a
Church.*[15]

_____ **Characteristics of Good Goals** _____

Since goal setting is so important in getting church growth
strategies off on the right track, it would be appropriate to
conclude this chapter with a brief list of the characteristics
of good goals.

1. *Good goals are relevant.* Be sure the goals you set
are the right goals. If church growth is what you are aiming
for, set 3-P evangelistic goals. Give secondary place to
how many hear the gospel and how many make decisions
for Christ. Give primary emphasis to how many disciples
are made, validated by commitment to Jesus Christ and
responsible membership in a local church. This will assure
that your goals are relevant to your overall purpose.

Also, as we have seen in this chapter, goals for the
future must be relevant to past performance. They must
be based on research, both preliminary research and diagnostic research.

2. *Good goals are measurable.* Before you set a goal,
be sure you have a measuring instrument available so that
you will know whether it has been accomplished or not.
The goal also must be stated within a certain time frame. I
mentioned that in 1976, Paul Yonggi Cho told me that his
goal was a half million members *by 1984.* Most church
growth goals, however, are set in a five-year time frame.

Accountability is also necessary. If you are the one setting the goal, make yourself accountable to someone other than yourself and God. Announcing or publishing your goal will accomplish this. Pastor Cho not only told me about his goal, but he shared it with everyone he could, including his congregation. He understood that an important dynamic of goal attainment is released by accountability.

3. *Good goals are significant.* Goals are challenges, but in order to produce a challenge the goal must be large enough to make a difference to those involved. In order to gain strength, faith, like physical muscles, must constantly be stretched. As the bodybuilders say, "No pain; no gain."

4. *Good goals are manageable.* This point is intended to balance number three. While goals need to be significant, they should not become pipe dreams. Constantly setting goals which can never be attained is counterproductive. While we should not be discouraged by a goal which we do not reach (Cho did not reach his half million by 1984, but he did in 1985), neither should we be ridiculous. We need to exercise faith, but realistic faith. As Dayton and Fraser say, "We are talking about the kind of faith which understands all of the dangers, all the possibilities of failure, all of the things that can go wrong and still believes that this is the way forward."[16]

5. *Good goals are personal.* Goal ownership is essential. The persons who are going to be involved in accomplishing the goal, in many cases the members of a church, must feel that the goal belongs to them. In some cases, but not all, this means that they should somewhere be brought into the process of setting the goals. In each situation goal ownership will be attained in different manners, but it must not be neglected. Two of the most recognized signs of goal ownership are commitment of money and commitment of time.

NOTES

1. Bob Waymire and C. Peter Wagner, *The Church Growth Survey Handbook,* 3rd ed., 1984. Available for $3.50 (postage additional) from Global Church Growth, 25 Corning Avenue, Milpitas, CA 95035. Faith projections are described on pp. 31-34.
2. Maxwell Maltz, *Psycho-Cybernetics* (New York: Pocket Books, 1969), p. x.
3. Paul Yonggi Cho, *Successful Home Cell Groups* (Plainfield, NJ: Logos International, 1981), pp. 161-62.
4. Edward R. Dayton and David A. Fraser, *Planning Strategies for World Evangelization* (Grand Rapids: Wm. B. Eerdmans Publishing Co., 1980).
5. C. Peter Wagner, *Your Church Can Grow: Seven Vital Signs of a Healthy Church* (Ventura, CA: Regal Books, 1976, 1984).
6. Paul Beasley-Murray and Alan Wilkinson, *Turning the Tide: An Assessment of Baptist Church Growth* (London: British Bible Society, 1981).
7. C. Peter Wagner, *Leading Your Church to Growth* (Ventura, CA: Regal Books, 1984).
8. _____, *Your Spiritual Gifts Can Help Your Church Grow* (Ventura, CA: Regal Books, 1979).
9. _____, *Your Church Can Be Healthy* (Nashville: Abingdon Press, 1969).
10. Eddie Gibbs, *Body Building Exercises for the Local Church* (London: Falcon, 1979).
11. Charles L. Chaney, *Church Planting at the End of the Twentieth Century* (Wheaton, IL: Tyndale House, 1982).
12. Elmer L. Towns, *Getting a Church Started.* Privately published at Church Growth Institute, Box 4404, Lynchburg, VA 24502.
13. David J. Hesselgrave, *Planting Churches Cross-Culturally* (Grand Rapids: Baker Book House, 1980).
14. Jerry Appleby, *Missions Have Come Home to America* (Kansas City: Beacon Hill Press, 1986).
15. C. Peter Wagner, *How to Plant a Church.* Cassette tapes and accompanying workbook available from the Charles E. Fuller Institute of Evangelism and Church Growth, Box 91990, Pasadena, California 91109-1990. (1-800-CFULLER)
16. Dayton and Fraser, *Planning Strategies,* p. 418.

9
How to Target Your Outreach

For the purpose of planning strategies for church growth, we can see the world more clearly now than ever before. This is due in a large part to the multiplication of research centers committed to world evangelization, one of the manifestations of the growing interest in missionary outreach in the United States and in many other parts of the world. Schools specializing in evangelism and missions are emerging in major evangelical seminaries and substantial faculties are being recruited to serve the increasing number of American missionaries and mission candidates as well as numbers of Christian leaders from the two-thirds world seeking degrees in the field. For example, Fuller Seminary, where I teach, now has 12 full-time faculty in its School of World Mission plus twice that many part-time faculty serving an annual student body of over 600. Trinity Evangelical Divinity School, Biola University, Asbury Theological Seminary, Southwestern Baptist Theological Seminary, Columbia Bible College Graduate School, Moody Bible Institute, Dallas Theological Seminary and many other such institutions find today's student bodies bursting with evangelistic interest.

In Pasadena, California, the U.S. Center for World Mission under the direction of Ralph D. Winter forms an umbrella for over 60 different mission agencies, organizations and activities concentrating on frontier missions. In nearby Monrovia, the MARC research division of World Vision International works in partnership with the Lausanne Committee for World Evangelization for the purpose of helping to define the primary targets for outreach. The Southern Baptist Foreign Mission Board in Richmond, Virginia has retained researcher David Barrett, editor of the *World Christian Encyclopedia,* to join the effort. Patrick Johnstone regularly reports data in *Operation World.* It is safe to say that never before in history have so many fine minds zeroed in at one time on the challenge of evangelizing the world.

What is true for foreign missions is also the case for domestic outreach and evangelism. The Church Growth Movement has been one of many contemporary influences which God seems to be using to heighten the need for strategizing evangelism and taking seriously the research necessary to do it well. National church growth associations have been formed in England, India, Norway, Thailand, Germany, the United States, Taiwan and other nations. Some of them publish journals, sharing the research they are conducting.

―――――― **The Challenge of the World** ――――――

The biblical scope for evangelization is nothing less than the world. Before thinking of specific targets for outreach it is helpful to grasp the whole picture. While statistics relating to world evangelization are not precise, some current broad approximations are not far from reality.

Think of the world population as 5,000 million or 5 billion. Of them, roughly 30 percent or 1,500 million are considered Christians. This includes everyone who, if asked in a world census, "What is your religion?" would respond, "Christian." Obviously this includes many nominal Christians who know nothing about a personal commitment to Jesus Christ as Saviour and Lord and about living a biblical life-style. I am told, for example, that the average Lutheran church in Germany today has around 3,000 members, but church attendance runs around 100, sometimes 200. All 3,000 would claim to be Christians and would be counted in the 30 percent.

It is estimated that something like 285 million can be considered committed Christians. These are men and women who are seeking to obey God and who can be counted on as a part of the force for evangelism. That would leave about 1,215 million who are Christian in name only, or who may be saved, but somewhat marginally so. Only God really knows who is in the Kingdom and who is not, but by and large these "Christians" are not going to help much in world evangelism. Most of them need E-0 evangelism as it was defined in chapter 6.

This leaves 3,500 million people in the world who are not nor do they profess to be Christians. They constitute our broad target for outreach. But strategic planning will recognize that they can be roughly divided into two groups. The first, numbering 1,000 million have been called "near neighbors." This means that they, in their own culture, already have a vital, evangelizing Christian church which at least has the potential to reach them for Christ through E-1 or monocultural evangelism.

The remainder, 2,500 million, are beyond the cultural reach of existing, evangelizing churches. They are referred to as "unreached peoples" or "hidden peoples." They constitute over 70 percent of the world's non-

Christians and are easily the largest block of world population when looked at from this perspective. They will only be reached for Christ through E-2/3 or cross-cultural evangelism. This is what is popularly known as foreign missions. In order to evangelize them, someone will have to leave their comfortable surroundings, learn a new language, eat strange food, adopt new customs and love people who may seem at first unlovely. Fortunately, as I have mentioned, the number of young people in America willing to do this is increasing rapidly. And they are being joined by a burgeoning army of cross-cultural missionaries recruited, trained and supported by third world churches. The first research on third world missionaries in the early '70s counted slightly over 3,000. Today's estimate is 20,000.

Happily, we are not propping up a losing cause. As the century progresses, the percentage of Christians worldwide is gradually increasing, due largely to phenomenal recent church growth in China, as well as in other key places. Every day sees approximately 78,000 new Christians and every week sees some 1,600 new Christian churches around the world.

_____ **The Challenge of the United States** _____

While America is a strongly religious country, evangelization is becoming more complex. Presently nearly 70 percent of Americans are church members (including sects and non-Christian religions) and 42 percent attend church or synagogue on a regular basis. Some 60 million consider themselves born-again. This still leaves a large number of unchurched and a wide open field for evangelism as our existing churches reach out and as new churches are planted.

The complexity arises in the changing face of the American population. While modern America has always been a nation of immigrants, only in the past 20 years has its diversity been taken seriously enough to recognize publicly that ethnicity is here to stay. The idea that America is a "melting pot" has long since been discarded by social scientists. The nation is better pictured as a "stew pot," where different cultural groups freely mix and flavor each other while retaining their own identity and integrity. Anglo-Americans, the traditional shapers of American culture, now comprise only around 30 percent of the population. Europeans and Blacks and Hispanics and Asians and American Indians as a block of "minorities" far outnumber them.

The Hispanic population of California is increasing so rapidly that at the present rate, sometime before the turn of the century California will once again be a Spanish-speaking state. American Indians numbered 248,000 in the 1890 census and are over 3.5 million today. Asians are showing the most rapid rate of population increase.

Minorities now make up a majority in at least 25 major U.S. cities. Miami is the second-largest Cuban city. There are more Jews in New York than in Tel Aviv. Chicago is the world's second largest Polish city, and Los Angeles the second-largest Mexican city. In fact there are more Hispanics in the Los Angeles area than in seven Latin American countries.

The United States is the fifth-largest Spanish-speaking country in the world. Immigration, both documented and undocumented, is constantly increasing. There are 3 million unevangelized Muslims and 2.4 million unevangelized Hindus in this country.

All this says that planning evangelistic strategies for the United States must now take seriously the challenge for E-2/3 evangelism as well as the more traditional E-1.

_____ **Targeting Unreached Peoples** _____

One of the most helpful concepts coming over the horizon in recent years has been the "people approach to world evangelization." This has given us handles on planning strategies for church growth which allow us to see our task much more clearly.

The concept of seeing the world as "peoples" and of targeting unreached peoples for evangelistic outreach first surfaced prominently in the International Congress on World Evangelization in Lausanne, Switzerland in 1974. As part of the preparation for that, Edward Dayton, then director of World Vision's MARC research division, compiled the first *Unreached Peoples Directory* and it was distributed to all participants. Ralph Winter, at that time a member of the faculty of the Fuller School of World Mission, established himself as the principal theorist of the people approach in his address to the plenary session of the Lausanne Congress. He made a strong case demographically and missiologically that cross-cultural missions needed to receive the highest priority in planning for world evangelization.

Winter subsequently took a fresh look at the history of the modern Protestant missionary movement and discerned three significant eras. The first era he calls "Coastlands." William Carey sparked this era in the closing years of the 1700s when he wrote his book, *An Enquiry Into the Obligations of Christians to Use Means for the Conversion of the Heathens*. Mission agencies began to spring up on both sides of the Atlantic and missionaries sailed to the port cities of the world, more frequently than not against great odds. In Ghana, for example, only two of 35 missionaries who went there lived more than two years. Despite the difficulties, it was an era of distinction and Christian work was solidly begun in numerous places.

Hudson Taylor was the person Winter identifies as the protagonist of the second era, "Inland." While Taylor recognized that the task had not yet been completed in the coastal areas, his vision was to push inland. He founded the China Inland Mission in 1865, and that was followed by such organizations as the Sudan Interior Mission, the South America Inland Missionary Union, the Africa Inland Mission and many more. Denominational agencies also began to move missionaries inland. National churches sprung up all over the world.

But then, by the mid-1900s, some mission leaders made an almost fatal mistake. They became so enthusiastic about the new national churches in almost every country of the world that they began to declare that the age of foreign missions was over. They assumed that the national church could and would complete the task of evangelization in each country.

This set the stage for Winter's third era, "Unreached Peoples." Key to understanding this concept was distinguishing between what the national churches might do through E-1 evangelism and what they perhaps might *not* do through E-2/3 evangelism. Since, as we have just seen, over 70 percent of the world's non-Christians can only be reached initially through cross-cultural evangelism, the age of foreign missions must not be declared as finished. India, for example, has many strong Christian churches. They trace their roots back as far as St. Thomas.

But India, in this third era, is no longer thought of as a single nation. Rather it is seen as 3,000 smaller nations, called people groups. Of the 3,000 only about 100 have Christianity in some form among them, and only 21 of those people groups have a significant Christian population. What does this mean? It means that in India alone there are some 2,900 unreached people groups which need cross-cultural missionaries to reach them. Strategies for church growth must be based on this fact.

It should be seen clearly that assigning priorities for strategic evangelistic outreach does not hinge solely on whether the effort would be regarded as E-1 or E-2/3. Once it is admitted that E-2/3 or cross-cultural evangelism is the utmost urgency it should also be clear that not all E-2/3 is the same. Some E-2/3 might be directed toward people groups which are culturally different but which already have vigorous Christian churches. If that is the case, and if there is any choice, sound strategy would channel evangelistic resources toward people groups which do not yet have even the beginnings of a viable Christian movement in their midst. Many are calling this approach "pioneer" or "frontier" missions. Globally speaking, it is our number one challenge.

——— Research on the World's Peoples ———

After the Lausanne Congress, 50 Christian leaders from around the world were invited to form the ongoing Lausanne Committee for World Evangelization. I was privileged to be one of them and later was asked to chair its Strategy Working Group. After establishing a partnership with MARC of World Vision, the Strategy Working Group began systematically to research the world's unreached peoples so that the targets for outreach would be more clearly defined. Edward Dayton and I designed a series of *Unreached Peoples Annuals* beginning with *Unreached Peoples '79* in order to make the results of this research available to the Christian public.

The U.S. Center for World Mission also concentrates its research on unreached peoples. A Global Mapping Project is now in place there under the direction of Bob Waymire, applying computer technology to unreached peoples research with the view of producing computer-generated maps showing, in color, the harvest fields and the harvest forces for any given part of the world. Their first major publication is called *Peoplesfile,* edited by Alan Starling.

For several years a spirited discussion was carried on among the leaders of unreached-peoples research as to the best, most workable definition of an unreached people group. A detailed account of this process is provided in Ralph Winter's chapter, "Unreached Peoples: The Development of the Concept," in Harvie Conn's recent book, *Reaching the Unreached.* Following a widely representative meeting convened by the Lausanne Committee in 1982, many have felt happy with the definition which emerged:

> An unreached people is a people group among which there is no indigenous community of believing Christians with adequate numbers and resources to evangelize this people group without outside (cross-cultural) assistance. [1]

While we are on definitions, it will be helpful also to see the definition of a people group. The same group, following the lead of the Lausanne Strategy Working Group, settled on the following:

> A significantly large sociological grouping of individuals who perceive themselves to have a common affinity for one another. From the viewpoint of evangelization this is the largest

possible group within which the gospel can
spread without encountering barriers of understanding or acceptance.

The "common affinity" can be based on any combination of culture, language, religion, ethnicity, residence,
occupation, class, caste, life situation or other characteristics which provide ties that bind the individuals in the
group together. The specific combination will differ from
group to group. Examples of people groups would be reservation Navahos, Turkish Muslim workers in Germany,
Afghan refugees in Pakistan, urban Aymaras in Bolivia,
Arabs in the Los Angeles area, Chinese restaurant workers in Amsterdam, Franco-Americans in Maine, the Korku
of Central India and thousands of others. Further research
might indicate that significant subgroups can be discerned
within some of the larger groups just mentioned.

How many unreached people groups are there in the
world? The answer to this is still unclear. Many have been
using the figure 16,750, rounded to 17,000, which is Ralph
Winter's estimate. Others say the number may turn out to
be 100,000 or more. Time will tell. Whatever the final
number, over 5,000 of them have been identified and listed
in the *Unreached Peoples Annuals* at this writing. The
exact number is of less importance than the concept itself
as a basis for strategy planning.

As we pray about the completion of the task we can be
encouraged by the fact that the number of evangelizing
Christians in the world is truly enormous in comparison to
the number of mission breakthroughs which are necessary
to complete the task. For example, in the days of the
apostles, those yet to be reached were something like
40,000 for each believer. Today we find only about 15 non-
Christians to each evangelical believer. The world's 285

million evangelicals will be found in approximately 2.5 million congregations. This means that there are roughly 150 existing evangelical (not nominal) Christian congregations for each one of the 17,000 or so people groups yet to be reached.

Many feel that this kind of research can be a great encouragement to believe that the task of world evangelization can, in fact, be completed in our present generation.

—————— The Cholanaikkans of India ——————

Unreached peoples research has been going on for over 10 years now, and happily, some peoples originally classified as unreached have now become reached. One of the most exciting case studies comes from my good friend George Samuel of Kerala, India. George Samuel was one of the participants in the Lausanne Congress in 1974. Leafing through the *Unreached Peoples Directory,* he noticed a group of about 100 persons called Cholanaikkans who lived in the Mangeri Hills in his part of India.

Later he found that the original information had come from a group of woodcutters who, in 1972, had discovered this naked, fair-skinned people living in caves. Some news reporters heard of the group through the woodcutters, investigated and wrote a story in the newspaper. The information filtered through the World Vision network, reached Edward Dayton and was included in the directory. George Samuel had never heard of Cholanaikkans, but when he saw their name, God laid them on his heart.

Returning to India, Samuel gathered some Christians together to pray for the Cholanaikkans. They decided to organize a new mission agency called Tribal Mission, and they sent out a group to make contact. After driving as far as they could, they set off on foot through the forests toward the Mangeri Hills. Swarms of voracious mosquitoes attacked them and turned them back.

On the second attempt they had some brushes with wild elephants, but they made it through. The Cholanaikkans were frightened by these strange people wearing clothes, and they scattered to the depths of their caves. When persistent coaxing couldn't make them come out, the Indian missionaries tried something else. They took off their shirts and pants, leaving some cloth around their waists, and approached again. With this, a few of the brave Cholanaikkans came out and friendly contact was made.

They discovered that the Cholanaikkans lived in caves because they were afraid of wild elephants. Their diet consisted of fruits, raw vegetables and wild honey. They did not know how to cook food. They never brushed their teeth, shaved, bathed or cut their hair. They covered themselves with pieces of bark when it was cold. Their language was a mixture of Malayalam, Tamil and Kannada. They were greatly weakened by disease and bodily sores.

An Indian missionary couple who could speak Malayalam and Tamil settled among them. They treated their sores, taught them cooking and hygienic practices, gave them medicine when they were sick, and showed them how to wear clothes. They began to share the gospel, and several gave their lives to Jesus Christ.

By the third year they had built a small church and, at the last report, 50 were attending regularly. Some were brought into the city to give testimony at the Tribal Mission's annual conference. Four of them are now training for the ministry in a short-term Bible school. Few Cholanaikkans live in caves any more. The whole living standard of the group has been transformed.

But that is just the beginning. Finding the Cholanaikkans spurred Tribal Mission to continue unreached people research in their area. At this writing they now have 44 Indian missionaries working in 14 tribes in the area. For example, the Paniyans are agricultural laborers resembling black Africans; the Kurichiyas consider themselves higher than the Brahmins and refuse to eat with them; the Aramadans, unclean and irreligious, practice polygamy and polyandry.

Tribal Mission is only one example of a rapidly growing number of cross-cultural mission agencies being formed in the two-thirds world, reminding us that missionary work is not to be associated exclusively with Euro-Americans. Many of the unreached people groups will be evangelized by Americans and Europeans. But others will be reached by Asians, Africans and Latin Americans. In Nigeria, for example, the Evangelical Missionary Society of the Evangelical Churches of West Africa (offspring of the Sudan Interior Mission), is now sending and supporting over 600 Nigerian cross-cultural missionaries.

With all the concern for cross-cultural (E-2/3) evangelism, it must be pointed out that most evangelism in the past and in the future is E-1. The statement "nationals can evangelize better than missionaries" is correct. The job of the cross-cultural missionary is to establish a beachhead to lead some to Christ, to nurture them in Christian formation and to motivate them to move out to evangelize their own people and multiply Christian churches.

While the numbers that frontier missionaries personally lead to Christ is small, their function is crucial because they catalyze the potential evangelization of the whole group. This strategic fact underscores the crucial value of missionary organizations specifically geared toward frontier missions. It is not the unique purpose of any other organization of any type to trigger people movements in all the world's remaining unreached people groups. Let us now examine that precise task more closely.

———— Stimulating People Movements ————

In many cases, the best way for the cross-cultural workers to strategize the evangelization of an unreached people group is to pray for, plan for and expect a people movement. People movement theory has its roots in the work of Methodist Bishop Wascom Pickett of India, but has been refined and popularized more recently by Donald McGavran. McGavran points out that people movements historically brought huge numbers into the Christian fold in Asia Minor, North Africa and Europe.

The Reformation spread through a special variety of people movements. "At least two-thirds of all converts in Asia, Africa and Oceania have come to Christian faith through people movements." And looking ahead, he says, "The great growth of the future is likely to be by people movements. It is inconceivable that any other pattern will bring the nations to faith and obedience."[2]

The technical description of a people movement to Christ is "a multi-individual, mutually interdependent conversion." This means that many persons simultaneously decide to follow Christ. They arrive at that point by a group decision-making process in which the issues are fully discussed until the whole group comes to a consensus. Many peoples use this kind of decision-making process not only for conversion to Christ, but for all important matters which touch the life of the community. One of the largest people movements in modern days took place when 8,000 Dani living in Irian Jaya, Indonesia considered the implications thoroughly and decided to burn their animistic fetishes and turn to Christ. All 8,000 threw their fetishes on a bonfire in a single day.

This kind of conversion seems strange to many of us who have been raised in Western society where individualism is valued. Western culture gives permission to individuals to make important decisions such as who to marry, what job to take, where to live and whether to accept Christ with a minimal involvement of parents and grandparents, aunts and uncles, brothers and sisters or close friends. Most cultures of the two-thirds world know nothing of such individualistic decisions, and the group rejects them almost by a reflex action when they occur.

The conversion of many a community or people group has been retarded by Western missionaries insisting on importing their own culturally-influenced way of making decisions into people groups that find the Western way impossible to relate to. It is helpful to contemplate examples of people movements in the New Testament such as "So all who dwelt at Lydda and Sharon saw him and turned to the Lord" (Acts 9:35). Paul and Silas said to the Philippian jailer, "Believe on the Lord Jesus Christ, and you will be saved, you and your household" (Acts 16:31). It happened. "He rejoiced, having believed in God with all his household" (Acts 16:34). These incidents reflect the way decisions were made then and the way they are still made in much of the world.

Research on the outcome of people movements has found that the most crucial aspect of the strategy is to make sure the group has adequate post-conversion care. If this is provided, then the spiritual quality of churches emerging from people movements can be as high or higher than those started by the one-by-one method. Even though a group makes the decision jointly, the individuals themselves experience personal salvation and are born again. Granted, there are exceptions and certain individuals who participate in a given movement turn out to be tares among the wheat. They are dealt with in due time, but their presence should not overshadow the tremendous good that usually comes from a people movement.

When planning strategy for people movements, it is important to understand as much as possible the social structure of the group and their idiosyncrasies in making decisions. Part of this involves appreciating their world-view and their legends. Sometimes a redemptive analogy such as Don Richardson's "peace child" will open the group to hear the gospel. In many cases power evangelism is called for.

———————— Power Evangelism ————————

Pentecostals and charismatics have been familiar with power evangelism for some time. This is one reason why, worldwide, they are showing the most rapid church growth. Power evangelism is proclaiming the gospel with accompanying supernatural signs and wonders. The Apostle Paul testified that he had fully preached the gospel of Christ from Jerusalem to Illyricum "in mighty signs and wonders, by the power of the Spirit of God" (Rom. 15:19). When Jesus first sent out the Twelve, He commanded them to preach the gospel of the Kingdom and to "heal the sick, cleanse the lepers, raise the dead, cast out demons" (Matt. 10:8).

For too long a time, those of us who have considered ourselves straightline evangelicals have shied away from power evangelism. But times are changing. An increasing number of evangelical churches, mission agencies and educational institutions are becoming open to the manifestation of supernatural power in healing the sick and casting out demons. It was introduced into the curriculum of the

Fuller School of World Mission in 1982 by John Wimber who has written a book entitled *Power Evangelism.*[3] Moody Bible Institute teaches a course on ministering to the demonized. Timothy Warner of Trinity Evangelical Divinity School began offering a course on power encounter in 1985. Many other institutions are becoming part of this trend.

My friend Timothy Warner sums it up well: "The issue of encounter with demonic forces is one which has understandably been avoided by large segments of the church. For most of my life, I was among those who steered clear of such involvement." I, along with my colleagues on the Fuller missions faculty, can identify with that. But we also agree with Warner when he says, "We can no longer afford that luxury." Warner believes that power and the power encounter are crucial factors in today's mission. As he targets the unreached peoples he observes that "in many parts of the world . . . people are much more power-conscious than they are truth-conscious. We may preach a very logical and convincing message by Western standards, but our hearers remain unimpressed. Let them see Christian power displayed in relation to the spirit world in which they live with great fear, however, and they will 'hear' the message more clearly than our words alone could ever make it."[4]

Fewer and fewer are denying the need for power evangelism out there on the mission field where numerous unreached people groups live day by day in fear of demons and evil spirits. But familiarity with the power of God can also be seen as increasingly appropriate for ministry in Western contexts. For example, it is reported that in France today more sick people consult witch doctors than medical doctors. The preceding description of the rising ethnic population in America indicates that new worldviews are being introduced to our own nation. Haitian voodoo, for example, is now a prominent part of Miami's religious scene. Eastern religions and cults are on the rise. Even large numbers of Anglo-Americans are influenced by horoscopes and the occult. All this calls for power evangelism.

_____ **Targeting the Cities** _____

Not only do we need to target unreached people groups when we plan our strategy for church growth, but we need to recognize that many unreached peoples are found in the cities of the world. A major socio-demographic phenomenon of our age, especially in post-World War II, is the urban explosion. At the time of World War II only New York and London had over 10 million inhabitants. Now there are more than 10 such megacities, and the projection for the end of our century is 25. Mexico City had fewer than 3 million inhabitants during World War II, but it is expected to contain over 30 million by the end of the century, the largest city that the world has ever known.

Raymond Bakke, the outstanding evangelical urbanologist who has been carrying on research under the Lausanne Strategy Working Group and MARC for the past few years, has identified over 250 of what he calls "world-class cities," and he has visited most of them. A world-class city is one which has over 1 million persons along with international influence.[5] The number of world-class cities is expected to rise to 500 by the end of the century.

Bakke explains how the dual targets of unreached peoples and world cities relate to each other. It is not correct to think of targeting either unreached peoples or world cities for evangelism, but rather they fit together. Bakke makes the helpful distinction between (1) the geographically distant unreached peoples, and (2) the culturally distant unreached peoples. Granted, there is a cultural distance in both cases, but in the first there is also a considerable geographic barrier.

Traditionally, the geographically distant peoples have been the chief target of those we send to the mission field. But in today's cities, culturally distant peoples may be living in any neighborhood at all, and we are frequently blind to their existence as important targets for sharing the gospel. A first step is to see them as legitimate people groups who must be reached on their own terms or not reached at all. Bakke says, "They will not be reached for Jesus Christ unless existing churches become multicultural by intention or unless user-friendly churches are started by and for them."[6] Anglo churches and other churches in urban areas should develop strategies for outreach which take the surrounding ethnic groups seriously.

Some ethnics, particularly the upwardly mobile, will want to become part of Anglo congregations. Some, the nuclear ethnics, will be reached only by homogeneous unit churches which gear their ministry to a single people group. Some marginal ethnics are in between and seek bilingual churches, especially for their children who are being assimilated, at least partially, into Anglo-American culture.

With property at premium prices in most urban areas, city churches should consider maximizing the use of their facilities by welcoming ethnic congregations. Some of these congregations will desire to remain autonomous and simply lease space. Some may wish dual membership, and some full membership with the privilege of meeting by themselves for Sunday School or worship or fellowship groups. Some may need temporary subsidies. Some may later feel called to move out and start a new church on their own. Flexibility is the watchword for urban church strategy development.

———————— **Targeting Whole Nations** ————————

While cities are increasingly important as evangelistic targets, the politically-defined nations of the world continue to maintain the highest profile in the national and international media. As the Olympic Games remind us every four years, the most widely accepted way of breaking down the world is country by country. With all the necessary emphasis on people groups and urbanization, our strategy planning for church growth must not ignore whole nations.

One of the most promising contemporary designs for strategy planning is the DAWN movement. DAWN is an acronym for "Discipling a Whole Nation," a creative and aggressive program oriented around church growth. I see DAWN as the second generation of body evangelism, pioneered in the '70s by Vergil Gerber. It incorporates all the characteristics of body evangelism described in chapters 7 and 8.

James Montgomery, the founder of the DAWN movement, defines it as follows:

> DAWN aims at mobilizing the whole Body of Christ in whole countries in a determined effort to complete the Great Commission by working towards the goal of providing an evangelical congregation for every village and neighborhood of every class, kind and condition of people in the whole country.[7]

Montgomery is a competent missiologist who understands and accepts the people approach to world evangelization. But he argues that the best way to get on with the job of identifying and reaching people groups is to motivate the Christian leadership of each nation to take the initiative.

The DAWN program, as it is being developed, is long term, extending over several years in each country. It begins with an extensive research project on the status of evangelism and church growth in a given nation, with the results published in a book in the national language. Christian leaders are organized into task forces to provide coordination of activities and accountability for results. A major national DAWN congress is held for motivation, inspiration, training and goal setting. This is either preceded or followed by regional DAWN congresses over a period of time.

Existing denominations play a key role in the process. Each denominational structure works within its own parameters for setting goals and implementing the necessary processes to attain them. DAWN does not tell churches how to evangelize or present a ready-made program for them to follow. It simply serves as a catalyst to maximize the evangelistic potential which already exists.

DAWN is more than just an idea. The pilot project was undertaken in the Philippines where DAWN-type congresses, overlapping with Vergil Gerber's ministry, were held in 1974, 1980 and 1985.[8] The results have been amazing. The Christian and Missionary Alliance, for example, planted as many new churches in the five years after becoming involved in DAWN as they had in the previous 75 years of ministry. The Conservative Baptists doubled their membership from 10,000 to 20,000 in five years (1981-1985) and then set a goal of 90,000 members by 1990.

The second effort was carried out in Guatemala with

the national congress held in 1984. Previous to the congress a book, *La Hora de Dios para Guatemala (God's Hour for Guatemala)* was published in Spanish. It revealed that evangelicals at that time comprised about 25 percent of the nation's population and that the annual growth rate of Protestant churches was 12.5 percent.

At the congress, church leaders from all denominations made a faith projection to raise the annual growth rate to 17 percent so that the evangelical community would make up 50 percent of the population by 1990. This goal sparked interest in unreached people groups among the indigenous population of Guatemala, because leaders began to realize that the overall goals could not be attained unless the growth rate of churches in the indigenous people groups were raised along with the others. A first-of-its-kind congress of several hundred indigenous leaders was the first step. Then separate DAWN congresses were scheduled for each of seven "nations within the nation": Aguacatecos, Chuj, Kanjobales, Jacaltecos, Mam, Quiche and Tactitecos.

This sort of approach to evangelism, mobilizing the whole Body of Christ in whole countries, is where the rubber meets the road in planning strategies for church growth.

NOTES

1. Ralph D. Winter, "Unreached Peoples: The Development of a Concept" in *Reaching the Unreached*, ed. Harvie M. Conn (Phillipsburg, NJ: Presbyterian and Reformed Publishing Co., 1984), p. 37.
2. Donald A. McGavran, *Understanding Church Growth* (Grand Rapids: Wm. B. Eerdmans Publishing Co., 1980), p. 336.
3. John Wimber, *Power Evangelism* (San Francisco: Harper & Row, Publishers, Inc., 1986.) The full story of the course, MC510, is told in *Signs and Wonders Today*, rev. ed., ed. C. Peter Wagner (Altamonte Springs, FL: Creation House, 1987).

4. Timothy Warner, "Power Encounter in Evangelism" in *Trinity World Forum*, Winter 1985, pp. 1, 3.
5. Raymond J. Bakke, "Evangelization of the World's Cities" in *An Urban World: Churches Face the Future*, ed. Larry L. Rose and C. Kirk Hadaway (Nashville: Broadman Press, 1984), p. 78.
6. Ibid., p. 75.
7. James Montgomery, "The Principles and Practices of DAWN," privately distributed, 1985.
8. This story is told in detail in James H. Montgomery and Donald A. McGavran, *The Discipling of a Nation* (Milpitas, CA: Global Church Growth, 1980).

Appendix:
The Lausanne Covenant

INTRODUCTION

We, members of the Church of Jesus Christ, from more than 150 nations, participants in the International Congress on World Evangelization at Lausanne, praise God for his great salvation and rejoice in the fellowship he has given us with himself and with each other. We are deeply stirred by what God is doing in our day, moved to penitence by our failures and challenged by the unfinished task of evangelization. We believe the gospel is God's good news for the whole world, and we are determined by his grace to obey Christ's commission to proclaim it to all mankind and to make disciples of every nation. We desire, therefore, to affirm our faith and our resolve, and to make public our covenant.

1. THE PURPOSE OF GOD

We affirm our belief in the one-eternal God, Creator and Lord of the world, Father, Son and Holy Spirit, who governs all things according to the purpose of his will. He has been calling out from the world a people for himself, and sending his people back into the world to be his servants and his witnesses, for the extension of his kingdom, the building up of Christ's body, and the glory of his name. We confess with shame that we have often denied our calling and failed in our mission, by becoming conformed to the world or by withdrawing from it. Yet we rejoice that even when borne by earthen vessels the gospel is still a precious treasure. To the task of making that treasure known in the power of the Holy Spirit we desire to dedicate ourselves anew.

(Isa. 40:28; Matt. 28:19; Eph. 1:11; Acts 15:14; John 17:6,18; Eph. 4:12; 1 Cor. 5:10; Rom. 12:2; 2 Cor. 4:7)

2. THE AUTHORITY AND POWER OF THE BIBLE

We affirm the divine inspiration, truthfulness and authority of both Old and New Testament Scriptures in their entirety as the only written word of God, without error in all that it affirms, and the only infallible rule of faith and practice. We also affirm the power of God's word to accomplish his purpose of salvation. The message of the Bible is addressed to all mankind. For God's revelation in Christ and in Scripture is unchangeable. Through it the Holy Spirit still speaks today. He illumines the minds of God's people in every culture to perceive its truth freshly through their own eyes and thus discloses to the whole church ever more of the many-colored wisdom of God.

(2 Tim. 3:16; 2 Pet. 1:21; John 10:35; Isa. 55:11; 1 Cor. 1:21; Rom. 1:16; Matt. 5:17,18; Jude 3; Eph. 1:17,18; 3:10,18)

3. THE UNIQUENESS AND UNIVERSALITY OF CHRIST

We affirm that there is only one Saviour and only one gospel, although there is a wide diversity of evangelistic approaches. We recognize that all men have some knowledge of God through his general revelation in nature. But we deny that this can save, for men suppress the truth by their unrighteousness. We also reject as derogatory to Christ and the gospel every kind of syncretism and dialogue which implies that Christ speaks equally through all religions and ideologies. Jesus Christ, being himself the only God-man, who gave himself as the only ransom for sinners, is the only mediator between God and man. There is no other name by which we must be saved. All men are perishing because of sin, but God loves all men, not wishing that any should perish but that all should repent. Yet those who reject Christ repudiate the joy of salvation and condemn themselves to eternal separation from God. To proclaim Jesus as "the Saviour of the world" is not to affirm that all men are either automatically or ultimately saved, still less to affirm that all religions offer salvation in Christ. Rather it is to proclaim God's love for a world of sinners and to invite all men to respond to him as Saviour and Lord in the wholehearted personal commitment of repentance and faith. Jesus Christ has been exalted above every other name; we long for the day when every knee shall bow to him and every tongue shall confess him Lord.

(Gal. 1:6-9; Rom. 1:18-32; 1 Tim. 2:5,6; Acts 4:12; John 3:16-19; 2 Pet. 3:9; 2 Thess. 1:7-9; John 4:42; Matt. 11:28; Eph. 1:20,21; Phil. 2:9-11)

4. THE NATURE OF EVANGELISM

To evangelize is to spread the good news that Jesus Christ died for our sins and was raised from the dead according to the Scriptures, and that as the reigning Lord he now offers the forgiveness of sins and the liberating gift of the Spirit to all who repent and believe. Our Christian presence in the world is indispensable to evangelism, and so is that kind of dialogue whose purpose is to listen sensitively in order to understand. But evangelism itself is the proclamation of the historical, biblical Christ as Saviour and Lord, with a view to persuading people to come to him personally and so be reconciled to God. In issuing the gospel invitation we have no liberty to conceal the cost of discipleship. Jesus still calls all who would follow him to deny themselves, take up their cross, and identify themselves with his new community. The results of evangelism include obedience to Christ, incorporation into his church and responsible service in the world.

(1 Cor. 15:3,4; Acts 2:32-39; John 20:21; 1 Cor. 1:23; 2 Cor. 4:5; 5:11,20; Luke 14:25-33; Mark 8:34; Acts 2:40,47; Mark 10:43-45)

5. CHRISTIAN SOCIAL RESPONSIBILITY

We affirm that God is both the Creator and the Judge of all men. We therefore should share his concern for justice and reconciliation throughout human society and for the liberation of men from every kind of oppression. Because mankind is made in the image of God, every person, regardless of race, religion, colour, culture, class, sex or age, has an intrinsic dignity because of which he should be respected and served, not exploited. Here too we express penitence both for our neglect and for having sometimes regarded evangelism and social concern as mutually exclusive. Although reconciliation with man is not reconciliation

with God, nor is social action evangelism, nor is political liberation salvation, nevertheless we affirm that evangelism and sociopolitical involvement are both part of our Christian duty. For both are necessary expressions of our doctrines of God and man, our love for our neighbor and our obedience to Jesus Christ. The message of salvation implies also a message of judgment upon every form of alienation, oppression and discrimination, and we should not be afraid to denounce evil and injustice wherever they exist. When people receive Christ they are born again into his kingdom and must seek not only to exhibit but also to spread its righteousness in the midst of an unrighteous world. The salvation we claim should be transforming us in the totality of our personal and social responsibilities. Faith without works is dead.
(Acts 17:26,31; Gen. 18:25; Isa. 1:17; Psa. 45:7; Gen. 1:26,27; Jas. 3:9; Lev. 19:18; Luke 6:27,35; Jas. 2:14-26; John 3:3,5; Matt. 5:20; 6:33; 2 Cor. 3:18; Jas. 2:20)

6. THE CHURCH AND EVANGELISM

We affirm that Christ sends his redeemed people into the world as the Father sent him, and that this calls for a similar deep and costly penetration of the world. We need to break out of our ecclesiastical ghettos and permeate non-Christian society. In the church's mission of sacrificial service evangelism is primary. World evangelization requires the whole church to take the whole gospel to the whole world. The church is at the very centre of God's cosmic purpose and is his appointed means of spreading the gospel. But a church which preaches the cross must itself be marked by the cross. It becomes a stumbling block to evangelism when it betrays the gospel or lacks a living faith in God, a genuine love for people, or scrupulous honesty in all things including promotion and finance. The church is the community of God's people rather than an institution, and must not be identified with any particular culture, social or political system, or human ideology. *(John 17:18; 20:21; Matt. 28:19,20; Acts 1:8; 20:27; Eph. 1:9,10; 3:9-11; Gal. 6:14,17; 2 Cor. 6:3,4; 2 Tim. 2:19-21; Phil. 1:27)*

7. COOPERATION IN EVANGELISM

We affirm that the church's visible unity in truth is God's purpose. Evangelism also summons us to unity, because our oneness strengthens our witness, just as our disunity undermines our gospel of reconciliation. We recognize, however, that organizational unity may take many forms and does not necessarily forward evangelism. Yet we who share the same biblical faith should be closely united in fellowship, work and witness. We confess that our testimony has sometimes been marred by sinful individualism and needless duplication. We pledge ourselves to seek a deeper unity in truth, worship, holiness and mission. We urge the development of regional and functional cooperation for the furtherance of the church's mission, for strategic planning, for mutual encouragement, and for the sharing of resources and experience.

(John 17:21,23; Eph. 4:3,4; John 13:35; Phil. 1:27; John 17:11-23)

8. CHURCHES IN EVANGELISTIC PARTNERSHIP

We rejoice that a new missionary era has dawned. The

dominant role of western missions is fast disappearing. God is raising up from the younger churches a great new resource for world evangelization, and is thus demonstrating that the responsibility to evangelize belongs to the whole body of Christ. All churches should therefore be asking God and themselves what they should be doing both to reach their own area and to send missionaries to other parts of the world. A re-evaluation of our missionary responsibility and role should be continuous. Thus a growing partnership of churches will develop and the universal character of Christ's church will be more clearly exhibited. We also thank God for agencies which labor in Bible translation, theological education, the mass media, Christian literature, evangelism, missions, church renewal and other specialist fields. They too should engage in constant self-examination to evaluate their effectiveness as part of the church's mission.

(Rom. 1:8; Phil. 1:5; 4:15; Acts 13:1-3; 1 Thess. 1:6-8)

9. THE URGENCY OF THE EVANGELISTIC TASK

More than 2,700 million people, which is more than two-thirds of mankind, have yet to be evangelised. We are ashamed that so many have been neglected; it is a standing rebuke to us and to the whole church. There is now, however, in many parts of the world an unprecedented receptivity to the Lord Jesus Christ. We are convinced that this is the time for churches and para-church agencies to pray earnestly for the salvation of the unreached and to launch new efforts to achieve world evangelization. A reduction of foreign missionaries and money in an evangelised country may sometimes be necessary to facilitate the national church's growth in self-reliance and to release resources for unevangelised areas. Missionaries should flow ever more freely from and to all six continents in a spirit of humble service. The goal should be, by all available means and at the earliest possible time, that every person will have the opportunity to hear, understand, and receive the good news. We cannot hope to attain this goal without sacrifice. All of us are shocked by the poverty of millions and disturbed by the injustices which cause it. Those of us who live in affluent circumstances accept our duty to develop a simple life-style in order to contribute more generously to both relief and evangelism.

(John 9:4; Matt. 9:35-38; Rom. 9:1-3; 1 Cor. 9:19-23; Mark 16:15; Isa. 58:6,7; Jas. 1:27; 2:1-9; Matt. 25:31-46; Acts 2:44,45; 4:34,35)

10. EVANGELISM AND CULTURE

The development of strategies for world evangelization calls for imaginative pioneering methods. Under God, the result will be the rise of churches deeply rooted in Christ and closely related to their culture. Culture must always be tested and judged by Scripture. Because man is God's creature, some of his culture is rich in beauty and goodness. Because he is fallen, all of it is tainted with sin and some of it is demonic. The gospel does not presuppose the superiority of any culture to another, but evaluates all cultures according to its own criteria of truth and righteousness, and insists on moral absolutes in every culture. Missions have all too frequently exported with the gospel an alien culture, and churches have sometimes been in bondage to culture rather than to the Scripture. Christ's evangelists must humbly seek to empty themselves of all but their personal authenticity in order to become the servants of others, and churches must seek to transform and enrich culture, all for the glory of God.

(Mark 7:8,9,13; Gen. 4:21,22; 1 Cor. 9:19-23; Phil. 2:5-7; 2 Cor. 4:5)

11. EDUCATION AND LEADERSHIP

We confess that we have sometimes pursued church growth at the expense of church depth, and divorced evangelism from Christian nurture. We also acknowledge that some of our missions have been too slow to equip and encourage national leaders to assume their rightful responsibilities. Yet we are committed to indigenous principles, and long that every church will have national leaders who manifest a Christian style of leadership in terms not of domination but of service. We recognize that there is a great need to improve theological education, especially for church leaders. In every nation and culture there should be an effective training program for pastors and laymen in doctrine, discipleship, evangelism, nurture and service. Such training programs should not rely on any stereotyped methodology but should be developed by creative local initiatives according to biblical standards.

(Col. 1:27,28; Acts 14:23; Tit. 1:5,9; Mark 10:42-45; Eph. 4:11,12)

12. SPIRITUAL CONFLICT

We believe that we are engaged in constant spiritual warfare with the principalities and powers of evil, who are seeking to overthrow the church and frustrate its task of world evangelization. We know our need to equip our-selves with God's armor and to fight this battle with the spiritual weapons of truth and prayer. For we detect the activity of our enemy, not only in false ideologies outside the church, but also inside it in false gospels which twist Scripture and put man in the place of God. We need both watchfulness and discernment to safeguard the biblical gospel. We acknowledge that we ourselves are not immune to worldliness of thought and action, that is, to a surrender to secularism. For example, although careful studies of church growth, both numerical and spiritual, are right and valuable, we have sometimes neglected them. At other times, desirous to ensure a response to the gospel, we have compromised our message, manipulated our hearers through pressure techniques, and become unduly preoccupied with statistics or even dishonest in our use of them. All this is worldly. The church must be in the world; the world must not be in the church.

(Eph. 6:12; 2 Cor. 4:3,4; Eph. 6:11,13-18; 2 Cor. 10:3-5; 1 John 2:18-26; 4:1-3; Gal. 1:6-9; 2 Cor. 2:17; 4:2; John 17:15)

13. FREEDOM AND PERSECUTION

It is the God-appointed duty of every government to secure conditions of peace, justice and liberty in which the church may obey God, serve the Lord Christ, and preach the gospel without interference. We therefore pray for the leaders of the nations and call upon them to guarantee freedom of thought and conscience, and freedom to prac-tice and propagate religion in accordance with the will of God and as set forth in The Universal Declaration of Human Rights. We also express our deep concern for all who have been unjustly imprisoned, and especially for our brethren who are suffering for their testimony to the Lord Jesus. We promise to pray and work for their freedom. At the same time we refuse to be intimidated by their fate. God helping us, we too will seek to stand against injustice and to remain faithful to the gospel, whatever the cost. We do not forget the warnings of Jesus that persecution is inevitable.

(1 Tim. 1:1-4; Acts 4:19; 5:29; Col. 3:24; Heb. 13:1-3; Luke 4:18; Gal. 5:11; 6:12; Matt. 5:10-12; John 15:18-21)

14. THE POWER OF THE HOLY SPIRIT

We believe in the power of the Holy Spirit. The Father sent his Spirit to bear witness to his Son; without his witness ours is futile. Conviction of sin, faith in Christ, new birth and Christian growth are all his work. Further, the Holy Spirit is a missionary spirit; thus evangelism should arise spontaneously from a Spirit-filled church. A church that is not a missionary church is contradicting itself and quenching the Spirit. World-wide evangelization will become a realistic possibility only when the Spirit renews the church in truth and wisdom, faith, holiness, love and power. We therefore call upon all Christians to pray for such a visitation of the sovereign Spirit of God that all his fruit may appear in all his people and that all his gifts may enrich the body of Christ. Only then will the whole church become a fit instrument in his hands, that the whole earth may hear his voice.

(1 Cor. 2:4; John 15:26,27; 16:8-11; 1 Cor. 12:3; John 3:6-8; 2 Cor. 3:18; John 7:37-39; 1 Thess. 5:19; Acts 1:8; Psa. 85:4-7; 67:1-3; Gal. 5:22,23; 1 Cor. 12:4-31; Rom. 12:3-8)

15. THE RETURN OF CHRIST

We believe that Jesus Christ will return personally and visibly, in power and glory, to consummate his salvation and his judgment. This promise of his coming is a further spur to our evangelism, for we remember his words that the gospel must first be preached to all nations. We believe that the interim period between Christ's ascension and return is to be filled with the mission of the people of God, who have no liberty to stop before the End. We also remember his warning that false Christs and false prophets will arise as precursors of the final Antichrist. We therefore reject as a proud, self-confident dream the notion that man can ever build a utopia on earth. Our Christian confidence is that God will perfect his kingdom, and we look forward with eager anticipation to that day, and to the new heaven and earth in which righteousness will dwell and God will reign forever. Meanwhile, we rededicate ourselves to the service of Christ and of men in joyful submission to his authority over the whole of our lives.
(Mark 14:62; Heb. 9:28; Mark 13:10; Acts 1:8-11; Matt. 28:20; Mark 13:21-23; John 2:18; 4:1-3; Luke 12:32; Rev. 21:1-5; 2 Pet. 3:13; Matt. 28:18)

CONCLUSION

Therefore, in the light of this our faith and our resolve, we enter into a solemn covenant with God and with each other, to pray, to plan, and to work together for the evangelization of the whole world. We call upon others to join us. May God help us by his grace and for his glory to be faithful to this our covenant! Amen, Alleluia!

International Congress on World Evangelization, Lausanne, Switzerland, July 1974.

Index

Bibliography

Following are Peter Wagner's comments on 20 church growth books for your further study.

Arn, Win and Charles Arn. *The Master's Plan for Making Disciples.* Pasadena: Church Growth Press, 1982. $6.95, 176 pp. One of the key concepts of church growth theory is to identify people movements which travel along natural webs of relationships. The Arns call this "oikos" evangelism and develop the principle in detail in this book.

Cho, Paul Yonggi. *Successful Home Cell Groups.* Plainfield, NJ: Bridge Publishing, Inc., Logos Books, 1981. 176 pp. This book, by the pastor of the world's largest church, is not just about home cell groups, but church growth in general. It is very practical and highly recommended.

Exman, Gary W. *Get Ready . . . Get Set . . . Grow! Church Growth for Town and Country Congregations.* Lima, OH: CSS Publishing Co., 1987, 144 pp. This takes its place as the top book on small churches, geared to encourage them to grow. It is full of practical insights and tools for small church growth. While written from a Methodist perspective, its scope is transdenominational.

Gibbs, Eddie. *I Believe in Church Growth.* London: Hodder & Stoughton, 1985, 319 pp. This is the most complete introductory textbook on church growth available. Gibbs, who is a church growth professor at Fuller, writes with a combination of sound scholarship and a style which offers delightful reading.

McGavran, Donald A. *Understanding Church Growth.* rev. ed. Grand Rapids, MI: William B. Eerdmans Pub. Co., 1980. $13.95, 450 pp. The classic textbook by the father of the Church Growth Movement, this is the essential starting point for any serious student of the field. Originally published in

1970, the revision has many allusions to American churches.

McGavran, Donald and Win Arn. *How to Grow a Church.* Ventura, CA: Regal Books, 1973. $4.25, 180 pp. In a question and answer format, McGavran sets forth his thoughts on American church growth. This is the best selling church growth book, with over 100,000 copies in circulation.

McGavran, Donald and George C. Hunter, III. *Church Growth: Strategies That Work.* Nashville, TN: Abingdon Press, 1980. $4.95, 120 pp. One of the best primers on the Church Growth Movement, this book also provides practical tips on motivating people for growth, training laity, helping small churches grow, and planting new churches.

Pointer, Roy. *How Do Churches Grow? A Guide to the Growth of Your Church.* Hauts, U.K.: Marshall Morgan and Scott, 1984. 175 pp. This book is as good a summary of the state of the art of the Church Growth Movement as is available. Roy Pointer writes primarily for the British audience but in a style and with a freedom that is very appealing to American readers.

Smith, Ebbie. *Balanced Church Growth.* Nashville: Broadman Press, 1984. 178 pp. As fine a brief, understandable introduction to church growth as we have. Smith has included discussion of the major areas of church growth focusing on worldwide application.

Towns, Elmer L., John N. Vaughn and David J. Seifert. *A Complete Book of Church Growth.* Wheaton, IL: Tyndale House Publishers, 1981. $12.95, 400 pp. An amazingly thorough textbook on various case studies of growth analyzing a number of approaches to ministry in American churches including a substantial chapter on "The Fuller Factor."

Vaughn, John. *The World's Twenty Largest Churches.* Grand Rapids: Baker Book House, 1984. 281 pp. Case studies of the superchurches of the world (including USA) with analyses of the growth factors which have made it happen.

Wagner, C. Peter. *Church Growth and the Whole Gospel: A Biblical Mandate.* Harper & Row Publishers, 1981. 200 pp. Taking the critics of church growth seriously, this book probes the relationship of church growth to social ethics in depth. It is a scholarly theological statement that brings new light to the issues.

————. *Leading Your Church to Growth: The Secret of Pastor/People Partnership in Dynamic Church Growth.* Ventura, CA: Regal Books, 1984. 224 pp. This is the first book dealing exclusively with how both clergy and lay leadership can influence church growth for good or for bad, depending on how they perform. A substantial chapter on lay followership is also a first. The book advocates strong pastoral leadership to equip the laity for ministry and shows how this can be developed into a positive growth factor.

————. *On the Crest of the Wave.* Ventura, CA: Regal Books, 1983. 195 pp. A popular book on missions telling what is going on in the world and the means that God is using to make it happen.

————. *Spiritual Power and Church Growth.* Altamonte Springs, FL: Strang Communications, 1986, 147 pp. The exciting story of the phenomenal growth of Latin American Pentecostalism is interwoven with church growth principles so that other churches can learn from that growth and hopefully experience the same thing.

————. *Your Church Can Grow: Seven Vital Signs of a Healthy Church.* Ventura, CA: Regal Books, 1976. Revised 1980. $5.95, 170 pp. Wagner's first book on American church growth has now become a basic document in the field. It is in its 10th printing. Over 100,000 copies are in print.

_____. *Your Church Can Be Healthy*. Nashville, TN: Abingdon Press, 1979. $4.95, 120 pp. A description and analysis of the causes and symptoms of eight major growth-inhibiting diseases of American churches.

_____. *Your Spiritual Gifts Can Help Your Church Grow*. Ventura, CA: Regal Books, 1979. $6.95, 260 pp. Written from both a biblical and a practical point of view, this book shows how activating 27 spiritual gifts can have a beneficial effect on church growth.

Wagner, C. Peter, ed. *Church Growth: State of the Art*. Wheaton, IL: Tyndale House Publishers, 1986. Sixteen church growth experts contribute to this major work, sharing up-to-date research and thinking on aspects of the American Church Growth Movement. It includes historical material, an annotated reading list and a glossary of church growth terms. Completely indexed.

Waymire, Bob and C. Peter Wagner. *The Church Growth Survey Handbook*. Santa Clara, CA, Global Church Growth Bulletin, 1980. 40 pp. This 8½" by 11" workbook is a step-by-step methodology for doing church growth research. It is the authors' hope that it will serve to standardize the recording and reporting of church growth worldwide.